Be A Baller!

Have It All.

Melissa Krivachek

WWW.MELISSAKRIVACHEK.COM

For information regarding special discounts for bulk purchases please contact melissa@melissakrivachek.com.

First Edition. ISBN #: 978-1495367113

Manufactured & Printed in the United States of America.

Be A Baller! The Blueprint To Have It All is a trademark of Melissa Krivachek Companies.

2014 International Best Seller in 3 Categories: Women & Leadership, Business & Management, and Teams

Dedication

~~~

If I could dedicate a book to myself this would be the one. It's a simple reminder of all of the insanity one must endure to live a life beyond their wildest dreams.

But, dedicating a book to yourself is a little crazy. So, this book is dedicated to all of the crazy, ambitious, incredibly passionate, and highly driven individuals. To those who never give up regardless of how many sacrifices it requires, how long it takes, or how hard it is so they can have it all, all at the same time. Love, Success, & Happiness.

CONTENTS

~~~

Be A Baller! The Blueprint To Have It All

PROLOGUE

~~~

What Does It Really Take To Have It All?

Let's be brutally honest; chasing dreams is not a simple mission. It's irrational, crazy, uncommon, ridiculously hard, full of setbacks, defeats, struggles, obstacles, pressures, adversities, anxieties, torture, loss of sanity, physiological and psychological pain, broken relationships, unbearable sacrifices, loss time, hand to mouth periods of suffering, consistent poverty, periodical insanity, and dozens more uncomfortable and un-desiring experiences, thoughts, and moments. Changing the world, solving major problems, and fixing the broken is not a task for the faint of heart. Creating massive wealth, encouraging generations, and living out your dreams is not for the sane man or woman! You have to truly believe in the intended outcome to see and touch a future that currently doesn't exist and bring it from imagination to reality and know it is going to cost you everything you possibly have to give and more. You need to defy the impossible, defy the fear, and overcome the failures.

I share this not to discourage you, because those of you who don't have what it takes will give up anyway. I have written this book to those of you who have the potential to achieve your dreams at any cost to help you to realize what it's going to take, and prepare and condition you to deal with the challenges I mentioned above and the excessive failure which will never leave you alone. I learned all of this over the course of my life the hard way, and I share all of this with you now so you can learn from my mistakes, my defeats, my triumphs, and my victories. Please know that anything worth having, any success greater than good, will come at its own time and place and with immense effort and struggle. Anyone can become a multi-millionaire or billionaire, own anything they desire, but be prepared to give everything to gain everything. Only the passionate, obsessed, and downright crazy, stubborn ones will survive the journey!

PART 1: Getting Started

Understanding The Basics

Chapter 1

~~~

STOP GIVING UP ON YOURSELF

As I just spent the day with my sister, now months away from the happiest day of her life as she prepares for her wedding, I was required to try on bridesmaid dresses. I absolutely hate shopping, and despise dresses, but regardless of what I liked or didn't like, it was just the two of us. You see a couple weeks ago I went home and the entire bridal party picked out the bridesmaid gowns at local bridal shop. The dress was gorgeous and everyone agreed with the style, fit, and color but when it came to the price everyone was afraid to say they didn't want to spend $270 until days later. So, it's a Saturday, and I find myself at David's Bridal in the most uncomfortable situation ever.

You see, I have no desire to wear dresses, try on dresses, or purchase dresses, because they make me feel completely insecure. I'm sure some of you can relate. As I proceeded to put on the gown, I realized there were no mirrors in the dressing room. The only option was to come out so everyone could see. Fearful and afraid about being humiliated, pissed that I didn't want to be in that size of gown, and worried about my mom and sister's reaction, I had no option but to put on the dress. Not because I wanted to, but because I didn't have a choice.

What happened next shocked me. You see I've been busting my ass to lose weight and I've lost 20 lbs. this year. I am proud of myself for losing that much weight, but it isn't enough. Then something magical happened. The dress was too big. Now my fear of being humiliated was completely gone, and this feeling of satisfaction came over me. I've struggled with weight almost all of my life. I've wanted to lose weight. I've tried to lose weight. I've committed and uncommitted to losing weight, but today as I realize how far I've come, I can honestly say there's no better feeling in the world then standing in front of the mirror and thinking to myself "Damn! I look good."

Am I where I want to be? Absolutely not. Am I where I need to be? Nope. Am I proud of where I am? 100%.

Preparation is essential to execution, and just showing up is not enough. When it comes to health and fitness, not showing up at the gym, not eating healthy or taking care of yourself shouldn't be an option. For many years, I came up with a million reasons why I couldn't, didn't want to, or shouldn't show up, own up, and do the work it takes to transform my body.

Now many of you, especially those who personally know me, are thinking I'm not a beauty queen, runway model, size 10 with a perfect body. You're right. I'm not. But that doesn't discount the knowledge I have about taking action and getting results. Regardless of where you are right now, if you aren't consistently taking action, going to the gym, eating clean and working towards a better body, then you've set your standards too low and I challenge you to raise them.

Lazy, complacent, out of shape, BS stories and excuses have never and will never work.

Earlier this year I wrote this post on Facebook:

"What have you accomplished this year that you're proud of?

Unless you are taking massive action you won't get results. Here's what I've accomplished:

*Wrote a book
*Booked 9 radio/TV interviews
*Got recognized by amazing leaders as a "prodigy"
*Lost 12 lbs.
*Became consciously aware of the food that was fueling my body and completely stopped the junk, sugar, pop, eating out etc... and focused on health foods.
*Started regularly working out
*Focused strictly on my genius and outsourced all of the minor details that others are better at
*Helped my clients get massive results
*Helped Matt (my coach) make the cover of Evolution Magazine
*Gained thousands of followers on social media channels
*Began blogging daily

Don't think 20 days makes a huge difference in your life or business? It can if you're willing to commit and discipline yourself. Be all in or not in at all."

It compelled some people to feel bad and some others to write about it in the hopes that I would listen. I wanted to use this as a living example and a real situation some of you may be going through. The following is the individuals' FB e-mail to me. The rest of the chapter contains my response. I have not altered their e-mail so you can feel the pain.

"So I just work up... Yep 11 am and saw your comments about all you accomplished in a year.. thinking to myself why is she putting last year's stuff on today with it being a brand new year..... read on.... And explored your page only to learn that you have already kicked some major ass and its 20 days in to this new year.... Wow... my immediate reaction was cool for her..... I start to make my coffee and say wait a minute that USED to be me... Mover shaker power house.... Now I am eating licorice for breakfast, yeah I am moving yeah I am stressed but my body feels stinky, I have loads of ideas and limited resources and direction and here I am again..... I have worked with therapists, spent money on seminars all over the world, read books, and been passionately in love..... And here I sit. At 57 feeling less than beautiful, overweight, having to catch up on taxes with drive and ambition but somewhat stuck and spending a lot more time on my iPad playing papa saga and candy crush then sending out resumes to regain my career as a MSW social worker and dynamic woman.... I am smart Melissa but I sink into myself, I get very passionate and directed and go.... And then within a few weeks I lose steam and energy...... So it's a cycle... Lately I am proud that when I do lose my focus the major fall is no longer returning to my former fiancée of 13 years and I don't sex out men or money to validate me... Instead I eat four bags of red licorice and sometimes Vodka at night as rewards for my stuckness...... I know I have at least one book inside me, I have been successful, I love money, I love the opportunities it provides, I am deeply spiritual in my heart and sometimes in my head and body but too often there are disconnects..... Want to write a blog of my journey, I have started once or twice, I want to return to social work and give back, I recognize how I feel and who I am when I am in that role.... I want to move effortlessly in my Bikram yoga class on a committed schedule, I want to wake up and seize those extra hours instead of remaining in my coma of (tired, and going to sleep at 3 am), each day... I want to take care of my taxes, my missing two teeth, I want to pay off my car and actually get the car I want, I don't want to turn to my kids to cover bills each month I'm late, I want to be the power house and the dynamic lady I had been once before and feel aching in my overweight body to release with zest and vigor... I am incredible I am strong I am a phenomenal woman and mom and friend and lover but I sink into so much less than that so often... I am BALLSY ... I have been told that, I know I am it is attractive in so many ways, I got things done, I reached for the stars, I had a mission, it was unconsciously innate my whole life and then I let life kick me in the big ASS. As I have repeated over and over here, I know, I do I get it ... But then I give up and loose it.... Only to start over for the 500th time, more frustrated, with more weight, less money, and loser mentality on my shoulders.... how do I make it stick... this has been extremely therapeutic for me, I have always been a writer and journaled and prayed and had a spiritual routine but even that starts and after 3 weeks Voila it ebbs into obscurity... So HI, thanks for the huge reminder and wake up call to stop the bullshit and be accountable and fucking DO THIS thing called my LIFE.... (Open to your feedback of course) With much gratitude and open receptivity ...I say a gigantic mwah and thank you for hearing me with your heart."

HERE IS MY RESPONSE:

No one can change your situation but you. You already know that, so the question becomes what are you going to do about it? Sorry for being so blatantly honest here because I know this isn't what you want to hear but it is what you need to hear.

How is what you are doing working for you? How does being fat, and lazy feel? How does being inconsistent and down on yourself feel? How does eating absolute garbage and drinking your sorrows away feel? How does lowering your standards and settling for mediocre feel? How does staying up until 3 a.m. and waking up at 11 a.m. shoving your mouth full of shit feel? It probably feels like shit!! So why would you do that? Why would you put yourself in that position to dig your own grave mentally, physically, emotionally, and psychologically?

Unless you want your kids to bury you knowing that you didn't take care of yourself, and choose to die instead of live, I would probably stop doing all the crap you're doing and tell yourself you've had enough.

Enough of the bullshit.

Enough of the lies.

Enough of the story.

Enough of the results.

Enough!

But really when is enough, enough?!

Apparently it's never enough SO instead of me preaching to you or judging you (which I am not here to do), I am simply going to do something with the hopes of it helping you. I am going to give you a kick in the ass. Listen to "The 10X Rule" by Grant Cardone. It's 7 hours. If it doesn't change your thinking, mindset, and mentality then honestly I don't know what will, because I don't think anything will.

Secondly, make small changes. You aren't going to change overnight so don't expect yourself to. You aren't going to wake up tomorrow morning and start eating healthy, exercising, and taking care of yourself so don't think that it's going to happen because it's not. But I do have a solution: start small. It's the minor changes that mean major differences.

Here's what you can do to change starting with where you are right now:

Go to the store and start with the basics. Fruits, veggies, tea, and protein. If you're saying to yourself, "I don't like those" well guess what I didn't either, but they slowly became part of my daily routine. Walk a quarter of a mile for the next week, then slowly increase that to a half a mile, three quarters of a mile and finally a mile. Drink more water than you currently drink. Start with a couple cups and work your way up. Decrease your caloric intake by a few hundred calories a day then you normally eat. It's the small changes that make a huge difference.

As you make these changes, you'll notice your mentality will get clearer, you will gain more confidence, increase your stamina and endurance, and feel proud that what was once difficult has progressively become easier. You will also notice you have more energy, increased clarity, and will sleep better at night. You will feel better, look better, and people will take notice. A compliment can go a long way and fuel your motivation to continue. When you do, you'll eventually reach your goals through hard work, commitment, discipline, and dedication. And, I hope you do.

Finally, I do sincerely hope that you get better, that you take care of yourself and that you quit giving up on yourself. Everyone deserves to tap into their potential, live out their life to the fullest, and be all that they were born to be. I don't know about you, but when I was fat, lazy, complacent, broke, single, hungry, and my parents were paying for my basic needs, I not only wanted more but I needed that freedom. I understand your hurt, anger, pain, and frustration. But you need to forgive yourself. You need to look in the mirror and take responsibility. You have a decision to make and only you can make that decision. I encourage you to watch the episode on Oprah's Life Class titled "Stand up with Steve." Hopefully that will give you the strength to start fresh, to renew, forgive, and move forward. It won't be easy, and it won't be cheap, but your life is worth it! I did it, and I know you can too.

This example is a perfect representation of what a lot of people have a tendency to do. This book is designed to get you out of this mindset so you can have it all, all at the same time. The best relationships, body, career, and self-image. As a result of following this blueprint, everything will improve. Clarity. Energy. Confidence. Accountability. Stamina. Sex. Productivity. And Profits. Then you can live the life of your dreams without the restrictions you currently put on yourself.

CHAPTER 2

~~~

GET REAL

Was I was scared? Yes. Was I lonely at times? Yes. Was I afraid of failure, rejection, and success? Yes. Yes. And Yes. But, you see I never let that stop me. I never allowed the fear of failure, rejection, and success to stand in the way of what I really wanted. If I did, I probably wouldn't be where I am today. I want to share with you one of the most important lessons I learned, because I used to lie to others and myself all of the time before I took responsibility for my situation. The following words come from best-selling author, Garrett J. White: (If you're easily offended by the "F" word skip to page 17. You won't find it anywhere else in this book.)

STOP FUCKING LYING...........TO YOURSELF.

Stop Lying about your Addictions.
Stop Lying about your Rage.
Stop Lying about your Hate.
Stop Lying about your Fear.
Stop Lying about your Desires.
Stop Lying about your Excitements.
Stop Lying about your Secrets.
Stop Lying about your LIFE.
Stop Lying about your Reality.

STOP FUCKING LYING...........TO YOURSELF.

Until you are willing to be honest about where you are and what you are feeling NOW, you will NEVER have what you truly want TOMORROW.

Consider that the reason YOU LIE to yourself and hence the world is because...

...YOU HATE YOURSELF.

Why else would you lie about what you think, feel and experience.

To feel embarrassed or shameful about any aspect of yourself is to HATE SOME ASPECT OF YOU...

You see the formula is simple.

HATING YOURSELF = LYING TO YOURSELF

LYING TO YOURSELF = LYING TO OTHERS

LYING TO OTHERS = A FEARFUL, SCARY LIFE BUILT ON A FOUNDATION OF LIES.

===> So the solution is simple.

Stop Hating Yourself Today <======

How you might ask?

STOP FUCKING LYING...........TO YOURSELF...
and start telling the #TRUTH at least to YOU in private, this is a good step in the right direction.

```
============
```
HERE IS WHAT YOU DO
```
============
```

Take a journal, a notepad or a camera and start with answering the following 2 questions....

1. WHAT IS THE GREATEST LIE I AM TELLING MYSELF TODAY?

Then follow it with.

2. WHAT AM I MOST AFRAID THAT OTHERS WILL FIND OUT ABOUT ME?

If you will answer these two questions honestly on paper and then speak them into a camera you will immediately begin to feel better.

WHY?

Because step one in LOVING YOURSELF is being HONEST with yourself.

Today you have one shot to reclaim your power and it begins with the simple process of telling the truth to you.

STOP FUCKING LYING...........TO YOURSELF.

Love and Light,
Garrett J White - The Master Coach Mentor

Why would I share such a passage filled with the "F" word? Because it's powerful, raw, real, and relevant. You can't get to any level of success and maintain it without building a solid foundation and that foundation cannot be built on lies. At some point, someone, somewhere is going to question your integrity, your commitment, and your honesty. If you can't back it up with facts, you will ultimately have nothing to stand on. Which will then leave you sinking into a deep depression, and it will be much harder to get out of then simply telling the truth.

Had I lied to myself and said that I wasn't scared, that I wasn't lonely, that I wasn't afraid of failure, rejection, and success I wouldn't have love, success, and happiness. I wouldn't be in a position to influence and inspire others to tap into their full potential and find their greatness. Honestly, I wouldn't even be writing this book, because I would be afraid of what people thought. The reality is, when you fail to step into your greatness with certainty you fail to create the love, success, and happiness you truly desire.

CHAPTER 3

~~~

BURN BRIDGES

The only way to create massive success in any area of your life is burn bridges with the things and people who hinder your progress and no longer serve you. Just recently, I fired a client who wasn't getting the results he wanted or should have been getting for the period of time that we worked together. While I wanted to help him, and I love making money, I understand that in order to serve both of us I had to let go, knowing that the decision I was making was the right decision. In business nothing should be taken personally. Rather decisions should be made that benefit the bottom line.

In my personal life, I recently cut off a friend I was extremely close with for the last five years. I struggled with making the decision and sticking to it because I've tried to cut him off many times before. This year I made a commitment, and regardless of how much I want to have his friendship, I realize all of the negativity, drama, bad attitude, and BS doesn't serve me or my clients and for that reason I had to let go.

Our minds are like a computer. We have 65,000 thoughts per day. 95% of the thoughts we have today we will have tomorrow if we don't change the input so the output can automatically change. Just like you fuel your body, you fuel your mind. If you fuel your body like a Ferrari then you will outpace, outshine, and outmaneuver others. However, if you fuel your body like a broken down pickup truck then you will be sluggish, ugly, and coasting along just to get by, hoping to make it just a little bit further.

Our minds work the same way. If you surround yourself with negativity, drama, and chaos, building doubt, worry, and anxiety, then you will never be able to focus, or reach your goals. You will always be pulled backwards. When this becomes a cycle, you get lost, confused, and upset that you aren't able to stay on track and progress towards reaching your goals.

In order to break the cycle you must burn the bridges that are restricting you from breaking free and moving towards your own goals, hopes, and dreams. Will it be difficult? Yes, but it will also be liberating. Opportunities and possibilities will open up beyond what you believe to be possible. Once you demolish the restrictions and limitations you've put on yourself and burn the bridges that have kept you from furthering your own growth and development.

Let's take for example the client I fired. About five months ago he begged me to work with him and was determined to turn his life around. At 50 years old he called himself a loser, failure, and let down. I'm not a therapist, so while those weren't issues I could deal with. I was captivated by his energy, enthusiasm, and drive all to realize that his actions weren't coherent with what he was telling me. I wanted to help him in the worst way. I took him on as coaching client for a small fraction of the price I normally charge. I was passionate about getting him results, but as time went on I realized I was much more serious about him getting results then he was and that wasn't going to work.

He had a coaching practice, was a start-up, worked a part time job, and had a couple clients. Then his father passed away from cancer. He's had a rough life. There is no doubt about that. I respected his decision to continue coaching during the grieving process and supported him throughout the journey, but every coaching call became a whining, complaining and bitching session and it drained my energy, sucked my time away and impacted me in a way that was dangerous to my business.

In coaching, it's imperative that you keep high energy levels so you can connect and resonate with your audience and clients in a way that triggers their internal drive to take action. It's also important that you qualify clients so you don't have to deal with the drama, chaos, and negativity which has the potential to damage your business, reputation, integrity, and credibility. I knew from the beginning that I shouldn't have taken him on as a client.

The breaking point was a text that came weeks after the invoice was due that said "I sent you (amount) via PayPal." My initial response was "Thanks." Then he sent an additional text that said something which I can't recall and because I didn't know what he was talking about I said "huh" to which he replied "Oh sorry. I'm just pissed right now." This prompted me to go into my back office and immediately issue a refund for the full amount with a note that read:

"Hey (his name),

While I appreciate you sending $(Amount), unfortunately I am going to issue this refund for the full amount and have decided to no longer work with you. I appreciate our time together. However, throughout the time we have worked together I haven't seen enough results or effort from you to continue our relationship. I wish you the best of luck and many successes but the investment on my part is worth far more than the return either of us is receiving.

Have a great week!
Melissa"

He responded "Thanks for being so honest. God bless." While I appreciate his response, if he were to come back and ask me to work with him again, I would decline regardless of how lucrative the offer was. You see, I believe that we need to make decisions on what is best for both ourselves and our business and not go back on those decisions, no matter how hard it is.

Maybe you've experienced something similar where you've had to cut off friends, family, or clients. When you cut someone off, it is much like when someone close to you dies. There is both grieving and rejoicing. While we are saddened by the loss, we are grateful that both parties can be in a better place and move forward. While I was building a business, there were many people I had to cut out of my life in the process. I can honestly tell you that I wouldn't be in the position I am in, had I not made a decision to do that.

The most successful individuals in the world understand the principle of putting themselves before others. This principle can make or break a business. See, you can't give what you don't have. For example, if you have hate you can't sell love. If you're jealous you can't sell success. If you're angry you can't sell happiness. Therefore you will never have love, success, and happiness at the same time you have hate, jealousy and anger. Emotions don't work like that.

In order for you to be a leader, to set the example and higher the standard, you must learn to let go. To let go of what's holding you back, to let go of the past, the hurt, anger, resentment, bitterness, helpless and hopelessness. You must learn what you truly want and what you are truly passionate about. Then you must go get that and forget the rest.

CHAPTER 4

~~~

ANYTHING TO MAKE IT WORK

I remember my client telling me a story one time that has stuck with me ever since. As he was filling up at a gas station in Dallas, he noticed a mother in a beaten up station wagon that shouldn't have even been on the road with a baby in the back. The mother, looking like she hadn't bathed in days, filled up the car with $5 of gas. Probably the last $5 she had, wondering how she was going to survive. As she went in to pay, a stranger from a nearby pump quickly swiped his card and filled her tank without her noticing. The baby who he could see through the window of the back seat was crying probably hungry, and needing a diaper change placed in an old worn out car seat with what appeared to be all of the mother's belongings placed next to him.

In our everyday lives, we struggle just like the mother in the story, to find happiness in some area of our life. We can find ourselves from time to time struggling to find comfort, security, and peace of mind. It is in those times that we learn how strong we truly are. How much we can truly handle.

The mother wasn't willing to give up on the child, and God isn't willing to give up on us. Getting the body of your dreams, building the financial wealth you want, being in an amazing relationship, and creating the success you desire comes at a cost, but I assure you that cost is worth paying. I share this story with you because the mother, although not in the perfect situation or condition, was willing to pay the price for her child. She was willing to give everything she had for the child. She knew that child was hers and there wasn't anything she wouldn't do for the child regardless of how hard the struggle was. She refused to give that child up, because the little one was her responsibility. She knew she would find a way.

Success, great relationships, passionate careers, financial abundance, and having a great body comes at a cost. It requires a ruthless and relentless commitment. It requires an immense amount of pain. It requires an immense amount of sacrifice. At the end of the day, when you look back from where you were to where you are, it is this cost that makes all of the pain worth it. As I look back at my own life, I can't believe how much I gave up, or how bad I wanted it. I have no idea how I overcame so many obstacles, temporary setbacks, and failures. I don't know how I stayed the course for so long, but what I can tell you is that those who want it bad enough are willing to do whatever it takes. They are willing to sacrifice everything they have. They have a ruthless and relentless commitment to success as defined in their own terms.

Will that mother ever live in a million dollar home? Probably not. But I can almost guarantee that she will make sure her baby has a home to live in, food on the table, clothes on his back, shoes on his feet, and an education. I'd be willing to bet that mother will make every sacrifice necessary to ensure her child doesn't have to endure the same pain she went through. I bet even though she won't get everything she ever wanted she makes sure her child does. It is this kind of sacrifice, commitment, and dedication that makes great people and great businesses. You don't have to be in the perfect place. It will never be the perfect time. You may not have the perfect circumstances. And, you may not have the amount of money you need but you will be provided with the resources you need to endure, survive, and eventually thrive.

CHAPTER 5

~~~

FUEL YOUR BODY LIKE A FERRARI

Nothing including -2 degree temps, people who don't shovel their sidewalks, snow, ice, or runny noses should deter you from exercising daily. It's important to put your health before wealth, or you'll end up spending your wealth to recover your health. I live in the wonderful state of Iowa and I'm sure that some of you reading this are laughing because you have no idea where Iowa is or you've heard that it's full of cornfields and cows. Well you would be correct. It's the middle of the mid-west and it has been a brutal winter. I have client calls to make, my biggest month in business ever on the books, and meetings to attend, but no matter what's on the schedule, there is nothing more important than eating healthy and exercising. Regardless of how many things I need to get done, exercising will get done. Not just when I want to or when I feel like it, but every single day.

Being an entrepreneur, it can be hard to fit in a regular workout routine. It can be hard to motivate yourself to stop what you are doing and to hit the gym or go for a run. It isn't easy to wake up excited about working out, but it is easy to wake up and be excited about making progress. I just got back from running through the neighborhood in the conditions mentioned above, and while I would love to say I was thrilled to be out in the freezing weather with a runny nose, cold cheeks, catching my breath, I wasn't. That run inspired me to write this chapter because it isn't always going to be easy. You aren't always going to want to do it. You aren't always going to have the perfect conditions or the perfect amount of time. That's fine, as long as you are taking consistent action on a daily basis to get the results that you desire.

Some people would say to stay in. Others would go to the gym and workout. While others would sit on their ass and complain about how they wish they had a better body, more energy, increased stamina, and the endurance to do the things they want to do. Yet those are the exact same people that are doing absolutely nothing but complaining. The sub-title of this book is called "The Blueprint To Have It All." "All" meaning love, success, and happiness. But, you see, you won't have the levels of love, success, and happiness you desire without exercise, eating properly, and taking care of yourself.

To demonstrate this point, let's look at different aspects of our lives where staying in shape is vitally important. Sex, for example, the more endurance you have the longer you can last. The better in shape you are, the more fun you can have in the bedroom. The sexier you look, the hornier your partner becomes. The more confidence you have in your body, the more confidence you have in the bedroom. I know what you're thinking: I don't want to talk about this. Guess what? I do. Because sex is part of our basic needs and an incredibly important part of love. Don't mistake love for sex though. Having sex can increase our desire to be together, but sex in and of itself doesn't necessarily mean you are in love.

Look, even sex can be exercise. It gets you sweaty, it works your thighs and gluteus muscles. It burns extra calories. It brings you closer to your partner, and it's just plain good for you. Who doesn't want more sex? Who doesn't want hotter sex? Who doesn't want to get sweaty, switching up positions, while screaming and making weird noises? There aren't many people I know that don't want that. They just wouldn't say it. So, if you can't exercise at the gym, exercise in the bedroom. There's no greater reason in the world then to use exercise as your ticket to get some. Don't take this as a ticket to sleep with whoever though, be safe not stupid.

Now, how about your business? When you look good, you feel good. When you feel good, you are more productive. A short 20 minute workout has me writing this chapter in far less time than it would've taken had I sat around and thought about what I wanted to put on paper. Instead I blocked out a period of time to exercise and the clarity surrounding this chapter has my fingers rapidly typing the message on the keyboard.

Workouts are not only healthy but they are also closely linked to wealth. Every day as I stare out the windows of this amazing 3,700 square foot dream home I just moved into, I'm reminded that the people who live in this community are extremely active and fit. Rain, snow, sleet, ice, or blizzards they are bundled and working out. It's the same people every day. They have no idea but these people are inspiration for me to workout. For me to get off my ass and take action. After all, who wants to sit on their couch and watch people run by knowing that those people are getting results and I'm not unless I get up and do the same.

It doesn't have to be something huge that inspires you. Eating healthy and exercising doesn't have to cost a lot of money. It doesn't have to take up a lot of your time. If you do it strategically.

Here's how you can make eating healthy and exercising daily part of your routine without all the stress.

Get disciplined or die a loser.

Yes, it is going to be difficult. Yes, you are going to have to put in effort. Yes you are going to have to get off your ass and go to the gym, eat clean, and take care of yourself, but that's a minor sacrifice for this thing called YOUR LIFE!

Every Sunday I head to the store and skip almost all of the dry goods aisles. There is nothing good that can be made from a box. Just like there is nothing real about the ingredients used to create the "stuff" in the box. My favorite place to start is in the fruit and veggie aisle. The cart fills quickly with broccoli, celery, carrots, spinach, strawberries, raspberries, and other fruits and veggies. But it doesn't stop there, because I'm a huge fan of meat and meat is great for proteins. So I grab some shrimp, hamburger, chicken, and turkey. I tend to stick to those four meats, but I also grab dairy products such as milk, eggs, and cheese. Occasionally I'll grab junk food like chips or Pepsi, because I realize I'm not perfect and while it's important to stay on track, it's also important to allow yourself periods of carb loading.

Once I return from the store, I take everything out of the bags and start making a disaster of the kitchen. Prepping the food for the entire week only takes a few hours and it keeps me on track to achieve the body of my dreams. All too often in life, we create excuses surrounding our goals and allow those excuses to take and keep us off track. Preparing your meals in advance doesn't let life or business get in the way. In fact it's one of the quickest, easiest, and most effective ways to reach your goals sooner. While I don't have the body of my dreams, I can tell you that what I do works. I just never put the effort into doing it consistently, and I was never committed to having the body I want as much as I am right now.

That said I spend 2-3 hours cooking everything I need for the week. Then I put the food into Ziploc bags and grab and go as need be. I never have to worry about cutting up the celery, or how long it's going to take to prepare lunch, or what restaurant I could drive through that doesn't have unhealthy food choices with thousands of empty calories leaving both my stomach and wallet empty. I don't have to worry about the unexpected things that get in the way, because I've prepared to deal with them well in advance. I also keep lots of water, detox, and dandelion tea on hand, as well as Isopure protein so I can feel full faster without all the calories.

It's hard to eat five times a day. It's difficult to cook meals that include proteins, fats and carbs. It's a nightmare to count calories. There's no doubt about that. Hell, cooking for one is difficult. If you want it bad enough, you will make the sacrifices, keep the commitments, and do whatever it takes, no matter what it takes to live the lifestyle you want. Every day, each one of us has a decision to make to live or die. I promise you all of the things that you put in your body affect every area of your life.

Let me give you a quick story to demonstrate the importance of living a healthy lifestyle, eating healthy food and exercising on a regular basis. I used to hate exercise, in fact I still hate sweating. I used to hate eating healthy, in fact I still hate cooking. I never used to care or take care of myself and honestly I didn't think it had any effect on me until.....I stopped drinking Pepsi, stopped filling my mouth with shit, stopped finding excuses not to work out, stopped getting in my own way, and stopped with the BS. When I dropped the excuses, the junk food, and the stories that I was "big boned" and started implementing the teas, water, greens, and workouts, my confidence, passion, productivity, clarity, and enthusiasm dramatically increased. Don't believe me? Try it for 10 days. Drop the crap and see how you feel.

The body is made of 80% water so try feeding it pop, soda, orange juice, energy drinks, and other high carb and sugar filled beverages and see how it responds. It slows down and eventually shuts down because your body wasn't made to handle that. Just like a gas car isn't made to handle ethanol. You don't fuel a Ferrari with corn and hope it runs optimally or fuel your body with sugar and hope it runs optimally because it won't, it can't, and it shouldn't. It wasn't designed that way. When you fuel your body like a Ferrari, it can run like a Ferrari.

Want to be sexier, slimmer, and stand out? Start making small changes that develop into habits over time. You'll notice big changes in your appearance, confidence, clarity, productivity and passion for eating clean and working out. It will no longer be a burden, but become your best friend. Statistics show that for every $1 you make you're leaving 30-40 cents on the table by not fueling your body properly. That means for every $100,000 your loosing somewhere between $30,000 and $40,000. And no one wants that.

CHAPTER 6

~~~

Get Your House In Order

Getting your financial house in order is a critical part of becoming wealthy. In order to understand and have a clear direction on where you are going, it's important to get clarity on where you are right now. I want you to take however much time you need and do these few things. Then come back to this book and I'll share with you the significance of these activities and the reason they play a role in helping you build the wealth you not only want, but wealth you deserve. DO NOT SKIP THIS STEP!

1. Make a list of every creditor you owe.
2. Call every single creditor you have and find out how much you owe down to the exact penny.
3. Once you have that list run your credit report. (You can do this free once a year.)
4. Compare what you now know you owe with what appears on your credit report. (If you notice any discrepancies, be sure to report them.)

Now that you know exactly where you stand financially, it's time to start doing the hard work to repair your credit if it's broken and to pay off your debt if you have some. And, believe me most people do. I did when I went through this process, and I'm sharing with you the exact steps that I've taken to get to where I am today. If you're like me just looking at the overwhelming amount of debt isn't going to motivate you to do anything. In fact, it's going to do the exact opposite. It's going to make you anxious, depressed, and stressed. None of those things are good for your health and won't help you achieve your financial dreams.

I want you to participate in an activity that will inspire you to take action so you can get rid of this debt, reclaim your life, and create financial abundance. Take out your journal, or a sheet of paper, and write down every single thing, and I do mean everything that you want to get in the next month or the next year next year. It doesn't matter if it costs 99 cents or 99 dollars. What matters is you want it, and you don't have it yet.

When I made my first list after selling everything I owned to make my company work, and still being in debt, I wrote down kitchen knives, forks, spoons, carrot peelers, toilet paper, garbage cans, mops, cleaning supplies, a couch, a TV (which by the way I still don't own), and a whole lot of other things. You're probably dying laughing right about now because who gets motivated by cleaning supplies and toilet paper. The fact is that I couldn't afford those basic things for the longest time, and those were the exact things that I needed in order to move out of my parents' house and into my own place for the second time.

I also wrote down every single thing I wanted to find in my dream home which I just moved into months ago. That list included stainless steel appliances, granite countertops, hardwood and travertine floors, a large outdoor space, multiple car garage, open concept living area, at least 3 bedrooms and 2 baths. The house I currently live in has all of those things and more. It's a 3,700 square foot property at the end of a cul de sac in a very nice neighborhood. It has 5 bedrooms, 4.5 bathrooms, 2 living rooms, 2 master bedrooms, 2 kitchens, and a 3 car garage. In addition it has all of the other things that I was looking for, except the open concept living space. However, you can't always have everything you want and when you find a good deal, you can't pass it up. Even if you have to sacrifice a few things in the process.

Nothing about being an entrepreneur is easy. If it was, everyone would be doing it. Sacrifice is a daily requirement in this lifestyle.

I still have a list just like the one above, and every time I get everything I want on my list, I create a new one. Generally throughout time, the list gets smaller and the investments get larger. Currently I have investment properties, a 2011 Buick LaCrosse CXL AWD red exterior with black leather interior, and an Audi R8 white exterior with black leather interior on the list. Notice I mention the specs, year, make, model, and other details. Knowing the details is the primary driving force behind using these things as your inspiration to keep getting out there, adding value, and making sales. If your list of dreams doesn't motivate you to pay off your debt and start building wealth, then nothing else will.

CHAPTER 7

~~~

To Be A Baller You Must Stop Majoring In The Minors

So now that you know the basics, how do you bridge the gap between where you are now and where you want to be? Stop majoring in the minors. You weren't born to be average or mediocre, so stop focusing on the minor details of your life that don't have any impact on the end result you desire. For many entrepreneurs and myself alike, there are things we do that we know someone else is far more qualified to do than ourselves. We let things that have little to no impact on the desired outcome consume more of our time, effort, and energy then we should. As a result, our outcome is negatively affected.

Most of us have a tendency to get caught up in the weeds of life with the things that have little significance. Here are three small things you can do to win in this game called life:

Focus on the vital few. Become the master at one vs. being mediocre at many. There is no extremely successful person who relies on themselves to master every aspect of their life or business. If you're a doctor, you probably pay someone to detail your car. Just like you have a staff of nurses, radiologists, anesthesiologists, and other specialists on call to perform surgery. If you're a millionaire you probably have a chef, gardener, house cleaner, and other people you rely on to help you accomplish all of the daily tasks that need to be completed. If you're an average person who doesn't have any of these things, let me explain why focusing on the few and not the many will help you achieve your goals quicker.

The most successful people in the world understand this principle and apply it in every area of their life. They understand cooking, cleaning, mowing the lawn, doing the laundry, or doing the marketing, social media updates, e-mail campaigns, or whatever else you need to do, will only be maximized when the right systems and people are in place. Why would you hire someone to do any of these tasks? Because it frees up your time to focus on the one task that you're the master at.

To take this even further you probably have noticed a lot of people have a tendency to add "professional" "expert" or "guru" to their name and yet they major in the minors. These people are far from "professionals," "gurus" or "experts." They are simply delusional about the productivity and energy levels needed to accomplish the things they really want in life.

Does it cost money to hire people, keep a staff, train your employees, or have someone come clean your house? Of course it does. But, it also costs more time, effort, energy, and money not to have them as part of your team. Growing up in a middle class family, we were required to do everything. Dishes, laundry, shoveling, lawn care, animal care, shopping, and on and on. I'm not saying this is a bad thing, because there were many valuable lessons learned. The most important lesson I learned is that it's better to pay people to do the tasks I'm not good at or don't desire to do, so I can maximize my potential and focus on doing the thing I am good at and get the most results in. That being coaching. This not only increases my confidence and capabilities, but it increases my potential and profitability.

This is one of the master keys to success. You are not now nor will you ever be a master at everything. Focus on the few vital functions that you are good at and build a team around you to do the rest.

Limit interruptions. Often times, my clients will tell me they don't have time. Well guess what. The clock doesn't care, because it still keeps ticking. Days turn to nights, minutes turn to hours, and months turn into years. If you're like me, then your to do list gets longer by the minute. The one thing I tell every single one of my clients is to focus on the one or two tasks that you don't want and do those first. This frees up your mind and increases your energy, but in order to do so, you will need to know how. For the next week try this: split all of your time into 90 minute segments. These 90 minutes without interruption allows you to focus on the task without overwhelming you. These 90 minutes must be focused specifically on the task at hand. If you are making sales calls, then don't have your kids or colleagues around. If you are writing, then don't have the TV or music on. Whatever you are doing, do it without distractions. It will increase your focus and allow you to get more done in less time. This applies to any area of your life, whether it be homework, financial planning, goal setting, sales calls, house work, etc... Your energy flows where your attention goes. It's far better to be doing one thing with a clear mind, then multiple things with a cloudy mind.

Here's how that would look:

Option 1: 7.5 Hour Work Day

Gym
8 a.m. – 9:30 a.m. Disciplined work
15 minute break
9:45 a.m. – 11:15 a.m. Disciplined work
45 minute lunch
12 p.m. – 1:30 p.m. Disciplined work
15 minute break
1:45 p.m. – 3:15 p.m. Disciplined work
15 minute break
3:30 p.m. – 4:45 p.m. Disciplined work
Leave Office and Enjoy Your Life!

Option 2: 6 Hour Work Day

Gym
9 a.m. – 10:30 a.m. Disciplined work
15 minute break
10:45 a.m. – 12:15 p.m. Disciplined work
45 minute lunch
1 p.m. – 2:30 p.m. Disciplined work
15 minute break
2:45 p.m. – 4:15 p.m. Disciplined work
Leave Office and Enjoy Your Life!

(Family time, gym time, date night, golfing, or whatever)

But to break that down even further to maximize your time:

Monday & Friday should be strictly focused on paperwork duties. Monday, when you arrive, you should organize your week. Friday, when you leave, everything should be filed and you should have nothing to think about.

Tuesday, Wednesday, & Thursday should be strictly fieldwork. That means making phone calls, knocking on doors, working with clients, or whatever. No paperwork should be done during field days.

After following this plan for 20 weeks, this is what you can expect. **(NOTE: This will only work if you work, and this is not by any means a guarantee.)**

Week 1: $1,000+ additional income		
Week 2: $1,500+ additional income	+$500	
Week 3: $2,250+ additional income	+750	
Week 4: $3,250+ additional income	+$1,000	
Week 5: $4,500+ additional income	+$1,250	
Week 6: $5,500+ additional income	+$1,000	
Week 7: $6,550+ additional income	+$1,050	
Week 8-20: $8,500+ additional income	+$1,000	

Notice these incremental increases have given you more time to do what you want and have increased your income $107,000.00. Do less. Be more. Have more.

Adopt a low tolerance for missed commitments. One of my clients who just transitioned from the world of bodybuilding to speaking had a tendency to miss every deadline he could. If he needed to get something done on time, he wouldn't do it. This tendency drained his energy and left him feeling unfulfilled. While he wanted to achieve certain things in his life, he wasn't able to until he set achievable goals with deadlines that couldn't be missed. If the deadline was missed, the consequence was significant. He went as far as missing his own book deadline which resulted in him having to push the launch of his own book back. An accomplishment he was and is extremely proud of shouldn't have had to be pushed back because he wasn't motivated to meet the deadline.

The most successful individuals in the world have a zero tolerance policy for missing deadlines, and I am no exception. Missed commitments lowers the standards you've set for yourself and allows you to do the things you want to do when you want to do them, instead of doing the things you need to do when you need to do them. Commitments are a critical aspect of leveraging your personal power to grow a business and become successful. Integrating these three rules in life will help you stop majoring in the minors and rapidly accelerate your growth so you can have it all, all at the same time. These three keys in addition to the 25 traits I'm about to share with you in Part 2 of this book will teach you how while providing you with all the tools you need to "Be A Baller!"

PART 2: THE BLUEPRINT

25 Things You Must Do
So You Can Have It All,
All At The Same Time.

Love, Success & Happiness.

LESSON 1: OVERCOME ADVERSITY

~~~

Use What You Have To Get What You Want

Overcoming adversity isn't easy. There are no shortcuts to success. Everyone is looking for an easy and cheap way out. True love, success, and happiness can't be achieved that way. As you will see from the stories throughout this book, I've been at the top and have had it all, and I've also been at the bottom and had nothing. In both circumstances there were invaluable lessons I've learned that have affected my approach to life and business. With overcoming adversity being the first of the 25 traits, you must have to have it all, all at the same time. Adversity is by far the most important. You should probably put this book down if you refuse to overcome adversity, refuse to focus on the habits and disciplines you must implement, or refuse to make the sacrifices necessary. You should put it down if you won't stop telling yourself the same stories and believing them, because the other 24 traits I share with you aren't going to matter if you can't master this one.

Overcoming adversity is one of the hardest and yet most rewarding things you can do to change your life. When I first got started, I heard hundreds of reasons why on a daily basis that I can't, shouldn't, won't, and couldn't have it all. While my friends and family are amazing, they also weren't the most supportive people when it came to the journey of entrepreneurship. Every possible thing that could be against me was. There were and always will be temporary setbacks, failures, and adversity. Not everyone is going to cheer for you or want you to win, so don't expect them to. Not everyone is going to want to take the same path as you. Not everyone, in fact, absolutely no one has the same hopes, dreams, ambitions, goals and desires as you. No one is going to understand your struggles and addictions more than you. But you see, in knowing that you will face adversity, there are things that you can focus on so you can overcome and conquer the very things that seem to be standing in between you and what you want.

Find Value In Your Circumstance. Growing up in a town of 350 people, being broke and in debt, driving cars that broke down quite often, and not being able to afford the things you want are the very things almost all of us want to avoid. Let's be real for a minute we would rather drive the car we desire, live in the house we love, be in the perfect relationship with the man or woman of our dreams, and pursue our passions. But very few people are willing to walk the road long enough or make the sacrifices required to attain these desires. There will never be a perfect time. You will never be in a perfect place. You will never be perfect. Look at where you are right now. Look at what you have right now, and what value you can add right now. Focus on changing your circumstances and situation by using the resources you have right now. No matter how far I've personally come, or how many setbacks I've had, those circumstances have blessed me with the opportunities to be in the situation I'm in right now. Focusing on what you don't have, and where you're not at, isn't going to help you build the mindset you need to overcome any of the obstacles that might appear to be in your way.

Encourage Yourself. Tony Robbins, Les Brown, Dr. John Maxwell, Dani Johnson, Deepak Chopra, and hundreds of others carry the title "Motivational Speaker". Yet motivation means, "arousing an organism to act towards a certain goal." Doesn't that mean we motivate ourselves? Of course it does! There is no such thing as "Motivational Speakers." Rather, they should call themselves, "Inspirational Speakers" who use the power of words to compel their audience to take action.

Inspiration means, "something that makes someone want to do something; a force or influence that inspires others to do or create." Therefore, the most disingenuine, inauthentic, title a speaker of such stature could give themselves with the caliber of influence they have is that of "Motivational Speaker." There is nothing Tony, Les, Dr. John Maxwell, Dani, Deepak or any other speaker could say to motivate you because motivation comes from within.

"Motivational Speaking" has gone on for centuries. The best speakers, authors, and coaches carry the title and yet the title, as attracted as we are to it, is complete BS. I've been in the personal development industry for many years, and every single one of the speakers I mention in this lesson I absolutely love. I think their content is great, their message is clear and compelling, and their events gross millions of dollars in revenue every single year. But that's the problem. While I love and listen to all of them, I can't stand the fact that we title them "Motivational Speakers."

The world likes to title people and listen to people with titles. Does anyone else see this as a problem? Let's face it, the problem isn't that we aren't inspired. It's that we aren't motivated. Most people are lazy, complacent, just want to make it to tomorrow type of folks, who love inspiration but aren't motivated to do anything. I deal with people on a daily basis and for those wishing, hoping, and dreaming of success they refuse to take action, commit, and motivate themselves to actually get shit started much less done.

If you've followed me on social media for any period of time, you realize that I personally post inspirational quotes and messages 10-14 times a day on average. Usually every hour on the hour. I get e-mails on a regular basis telling me how awesome my posts are, and how my fans look forward to seeing my posts to keep them going throughout the day. But look, it isn't the posts that have any effect; it's the way the posts are interpreted by the person reading them that truly have the effect. I can have a shitty day and no matter how much inspiration I read, I might still complain about how sucky my life is because I'm not motivated to take action.

So let me be clear. These speakers aren't motivating you. They are inspiring you to take action. They are living life by design, creating results, and INSPIRING you to do the same.

Let me give you an example: I just got off the phone with my coach, Matthew Lee, and while he wasn't as excited about my latest idea as I was, he asked me, "On a scale of 1-10, how well do you think this will work?" I immediately, before he even finished the question, said in a loud voice, "10." He followed with, "From your tone of voice, I'd say you believe 11 or 12, but the point is what you're doing is experimental not proven." I rebuttled with, "That's not the point." To which we got into a somewhat heated debate, laughing the entire time. This only motivated me to do it more, because while I respect his advice, in my heart, I know that it will work. Experimental or not, it lit a fire within me to prove him wrong. I love when people tell me it won't work. It sparks a deeper desire to make it work. I motivate myself to prove people wrong, and I suspect you might do the same.

If you've ever been to any events by the speakers mentioned, then you know as well as I do you weren't motivated when you got in there, and you certainly weren't motivated when you left, unless something was said that triggered an emotional reaction which sparked you to take immediate action. You can see now that it wasn't motivation, rather inspiration that got you to take action. There is no such thing as a "Motivational Speaker."

Be Consistent. No matter what actions you're taking, if they're the right actions there will be a payoff. You see, it isn't heroic feats or grand acts of bravery that get results, but daily, small, consistent actions. There is no such thing as overnight success. The only way to sustainable success is taking consistent actions. In order for there to be a payoff, your actions must be the right actions. Let me give you an example: let's say you want to lose weight and get in shape. Going to the gym once a year isn't going to get you the body of your dreams. Eating healthy whenever you feel like it isn't going to get you the results you desire. So taking action isn't enough unless of course it's the right action.

Focus on the small daily habits and disciplines required, and notice I said the word "required" to help you stay on course and get the results you want. If you want a great body, then consistently workout, consistently eat clean, and consistently hold yourself accountable. If you want to build a bigger business, consistently focus on prospecting, consistently pick up the phone and make sales, consistently look at where your time is being spent and if your time is being spent wisely. I stress the word "consistently", and use it A LOT to make sure you understand that the only way to get the results you want is to be consistent.

Prepare. Showing up isn't enough. People make an appearance all the time, but that doesn't mean they win *American Idol* or land the job of their dreams. The most successful people aren't even the best educated or the most knowledgeable but they are the ones who have spent the most time preparing. Preparation is essential when it comes to overcoming adversity. Having a list of goals isn't enough. We all make lists, but how many of us actually accomplish the things on those lists. Very few. Preparation means putting in the time necessary to learn the knowledge, getting access to the resources, building the relationships, creating the plan, and setting the pace for you to execute it.

Execute. Once you have the tools, knowledge, resources, and plan, you can now begin to execute in the quickest, easiest, most effective and profitable way possible. Execution again requires consistency, but because we've already talked about that and hopefully you've already started implementing that, all you will need to do is show up and deliver. Execution is the key to true, sustainable results.

Let me end this lesson with an example from my own personal life. For years, I've been looking up to and studying some of the best personal development speakers and leaders in the world. This year, I've had the opportunity to be on tele-seminars and collaborate working side by side with these leaders because I not only found value in the worst possible circumstances, but I integrated every single habit and discipline I talk about in this book. So, when I showed up my message was clear, my passion was noticeable, and my presence spoke louder than my presentation. No matter where you are in your business or life, no matter how many things are standing in the way of love, success, and happiness, you too can have it all, all at the same time if you learn to overcome adversity.

LESSON 2: BREAK BAD HABITS

~~~

The Definition Of Insanity Is Doing The Same Thing Over And Over, Expecting A Different Result

I just finished doing an interview with Darren Casey of Get Lean PT in the UK. Darren has been in the fitness industry for 15 years and travels the world helping people lose weight and get lean. He has 18 certifications, has done 20,000+ consultations, and has burned more than 200,000+ lbs. of fat. Let me just be totally honest I've struggled with weight for the majority of my life, but this year I've decided to take control and break the habits that I've developed from childhood and carried into adulthood. I am doing this so I can look sexier and be healthier than I've ever been. I've talked about having personal trainers as my coaching clients before, and while I've implemented their advice and it worked, I wasn't fully committed to taking the exact actions or making the sacrifices and creating the habits and disciplines necessary to have the body of my dreams until I hired Darren.

This lesson is one of the hardest for me to talk about and deal with, because I, like everyone else, have developed habits that aren't healthy and aren't easy to overcome. Maybe weight isn't an issue for you, but instead you've developed habits like smoking, chewing, drinking alcohol, doing drugs, biting your nails, speeding, etc... Whatever your secret addiction is, it's time to stop that shit, and quit letting others enable you to continue. This will probably be one of the funniest chapters In this book, and I guarantee the lesson I share with you will make you talk about it for days because while it's funny, it's also true and you'll be glad it didn't happen to you.

This isn't the first time I've had to break habits, and it isn't the last. There are three keys to breaking bad habits, and as much as I don't want to tell this story, I'm going to because it's going to drive the point home. It's an extreme case of what can happen when you don't break the habits you know you shouldn't have started to begin with.

As an entrepreneur and strong headed female, I hated the law but that doesn't mean I don't have to follow it. For years, no matter what it cost, I would speed when I was driving. I didn't care if I got tickets. I didn't care if it cost money. I didn't care if I had my license taken away. I just didn't give a shit. Period.

Know Your Triggers. No matter what car I drove, what state I was in, or how old I was, for about 7 years I had absolutely zero respect for the no speeding law. When it came to paying tolls, I could've cared less. After all, why should I pay to drive on the roads when I didn't live or register my vehicle with that state? Hell, I went as far as not insuring my car, and driving without a license. Before I tell you what triggered this madness, I should tell you that I have learned an invaluable, and extremely costly lesson. I've never liked rules, never followed rules, and think rules are meant to be broken except this one, but only because as you'll see, it wasn't worth paying for. Ever since I was little, I didn't want to be told what to do and if someone wanted to tell me what to do, I would do the exact opposite.

Get Caught. In order to change you must get caught. While most people learn the first time they get caught, I didn't. In fact, I've probably had my license taken away at least 7 times. Because not only did I get caught, I chose not to pay the price. How dare someone tell me the law and then charge me for not following it. I wasn't just caught once speeding. I was caught over, and over, and over. Honestly, no matter how many times I was caught and how much money I owed multiple states I still didn't care until, I had to pay the price.

Pay The Price. I knew I had a speeding problem. I knew what triggered it, and I knew I was going to keep getting tickets but that still didn't stop me. It wasn't until 36 speeding tickets later that the judge was a complete asshole, and sent me to jail for 6 days for speeding and not paying the fines accrued. I didn't have anything on my record but speeding. The first time I went to jail for an hour or so until my mom could come get me and pay to get the car out of impound. The second time, I went for 2 days and that still didn't stop me because there were people to talk to and things to do. The third time, I went for 4 days and it was the most miserable experience of my life. I've done a lot of things, but there is absolutely nothing that compares to spending 4 days by yourself in basically solitary confinement with no technology, friends, conversations, television, or good food then spending time in jail. What I'm going to tell you isn't going to be pretty and it isn't something I'm proud of and it definitely isn't something I will EVER do again because the price it cost wasn't worth paying.

I've spent tens of thousands of dollars (that's no exaggeration) in tickets, court costs, impound fees, licensing exams, and SR-22 insurance which I no longer have to carry. Yes I have a valid license. Yes I'm adamant about properly registering my car and fully insuring it. More importantly, yes I've learned my lesson and I hope it's one you never have to experience because I wouldn't wish it on anyone.

The four days I spent in jail was the absolute breaking point for me. That's when I broke down mentally, physically, emotionally, and psychologically. I spent hours and hours those four days looking in the mirror crying wondering who this person I became was. Day one I got my period. Day two I got food poisoning. It was lonely. It was beyond miserable. It was the absolute worst time of my life. I can't stress that enough. But, if I hadn't gone through this experience, I wouldn't be where I am. I wouldn't have what I have. And, I wouldn't be telling these stories, so you can learn that breaking habits is NOT easy. It's going to cost you and it can cost you everything if you don't make the change including your freedom and your life.

Once I made the decision to stop speeding, which only happened because of the consequences I had to face, I began traveling again after nearly two years without a license. However, my speeding habit then turned into a "Why should I pay to drive on Illinois roads and pay tolls when I don't live or register my vehicle with this state?" So, just like speeding, in three days I got 27 fines and paid $739.20 in toll fees. Obviously by now, this whole not following the law thing was out of control. The law is the law to protect you. It's not optional. No matter how cool you think you are or how much you think you don't have to follow it, or how deep your pockets are I can promise you this: There are no exceptions.

It's funny for a while, but once you've paid an extreme price for stupidity like I did, you learn these habits aren't worth keeping. We all have bad habits. There isn't a single one of us who doesn't. Maybe your habits aren't going to cost you what mine did, but if you don't know your triggers and you're enabling someone else's bad habits knock that shit off! And, knock it off now. There is no reason for you to be an enabler. You aren't helping that person overcome their habit and more importantly you aren't helping yourself. As for my other bad habits, like consuming too much Pepsi, the consequences aren't so extreme. Darren has become my go to guy, my accountability partner, and coach along the way to achieving the body I desire. Find someone like that in your life to help you break through your bad habits.

The point of this lesson is to encourage you to look at your own life and evaluate your own habits. What are you doing that you know you shouldn't be? What activities are you engaging in that aren't benefiting you? What negative habits have you developed and what's your plan to overcome them? Don't let these habits take away your freedom or your life. Find out what they are, know what triggers them, ask for help, get someone to hold you accountable, invest in yourself because your life is worth it, get rid of the enablers, and change your habits to something that will benefit both your life and your business. Believe me when I say, "It's worth it!"

LESSON 3: BUILD SOLID LONG-TERM RELATIONSHIPS

~~~

Listen, Ask Questions & Add Value

Relationships are the backbone of business and one of the greatest assets a person has. Sitting with some of the most brilliant minds in the world and having a conversation, it's evident that they didn't get to where they are on their own. In fact, if you've ever been to their office or home you will notice a huge rolodex with prominent names most of us wish we had access to and the truth of the matter is, their entire success was built around hard work and great relationships.

But why should you care? As a small business, your greatest asset isn't your time, effort, energy or the amount of money you've put into the business but rather the relationships you've built with the people who support you. I want to challenge you to go through the assets you currently have available, such as your FB friends or Fans, LinkedIn Connections, Twitter Followers, YouTube Subscribers, Phone Contacts, etc... those individuals are connected to you because they have a vested interest in the value you bring to the market place. As you go through this list of individuals, build strategic relationships with those who have the largest impact in your specific industry and throughout time you will realize the significance of your investment because the return is far greater than you anticipate.

One of the greatest ways I've learned to build relationships is to listen, but more importantly ask questions. I've had conversations with multi-millionaires of all ages and no matter how much money they've made, how old they are, or what level of success they've achieved, they are always looking for ways to grow, get more exposure, and add more money to the bottom line. The key to having a successful conversation is to focus on how you can add value to the person's life. No one loves talking about anything more than they love to talk about themselves. Therefore, when you listen, ask questions, and add value, you stick out.

Let me give you an example: I was speaking with a leader who has more than a million people on his e-mail list. He has more than 400 affiliates promoting his content. He has his book translated into more than 15 languages. And, he's spent the last 25 years traveling the globe and inspiring more than 70 million individuals. He's received prestigious awards and accolades from the President of the US, Congress, and various other organizations for his speaking and leadership ability. So, how could I possibly add value to this individual who has achieved such a significant amount of success in his life and business? The answer came when I asked a simple question "How many people do you want to influence?" His response "I'm 65, but I want to leave a legacy for generations. I'd like to influence 300 million people."

I have some incredible connections and while he was trying to sell me on letting him help me grow and expand my business. He ended up selling himself on letting me help him grow and expand his business. After multiple conversations with this individual, I've been able to connect him with some great people, other than myself, that can help him reach his goals in the quickest, easiest, most effective, and profitable way possible. Building these relationships isn't as difficult as we tend to think. The key is to focus on the individual we are speaking with and not ourselves.

Here are a couple tips to help you navigate the waters so you too can connect with some amazing individuals you aspire to be like who are making the money you want to make, and creating the impact you want to have.

Be Resourceful. The greatest asset I've utilized to build amazing relationships is the power of social media. I'm very particular about what I use though. Instead of focusing on how many platforms I can sign up for and not be active on. I choose three to be very active on Facebook, LinkedIn, and Twitter.

Facebook is good for a couple things. First and most importantly you can participate in groups. The more value a person brings to a group, the more valuable the individual becomes. As I study the information the individual is providing, I decide whether or not to reach out and send a friend connection. I also make a point not to participate in groups or "like" pages unless I can add or extract value from participating in that particular group or page. There is no point in "liking" hundreds of pages or being involved in hundreds of groups like many people do if you aren't connecting with those who empower and inspire you to take action, tap into your full potential, and be greater than you already are.

Twitter I use in several ways. For those who have too many fans on FB, I'll use Twitter because it isn't likely that both of those platforms are maximizing their potential for the individual. For example on FB, Max Philsaire, a fitness professional, elite competitor and Hollywood trainer has 1,069,533 likes and that's more than likely increased by the time you read this book. With that many "likes" it's impossible to respond to each comment individually. However, if you visit his Twitter handle, he has 3,850 followers. Because I've done the research and know this I've been able to have personal conversations with Max. I would have never got his attention on FB based strictly on the numbers. Now, if someone has tens of thousands of followers on twitter and not on their FB page then I'll use FB to reach out and connect. Go where there is the least resistance and fewer number of people trying to connect with the individual you are interested in connecting with. You'll have a better chance at building a relationship with them.

LinkedIn is the final platform I use, because it's designed for serious professionals who are looking to grow their network and their business. Almost always, individuals from Twitter will connect with me there. There are a couple things that you should know about LinkedIn though, so you can maximize its purpose and build a strong network of individuals who value relationships as much as you do. When you design your profile, list the things that clients come to you for. Your profile is designed to help people find what they are looking for. If all you do is talk about yourself and how awesome you are, no one is going to be attracted, much less have the desire to talk to or buy from you. Just like in sales, your LinkedIn profile is a soft pitch to get the viewers interested in what you do. Enough so that they reach out ask questions, and give you the opportunity to add value while possibly closing them.

Be Genuine. When you connect with powerful players in any industry, listen to what they are saying and actually care. Over the last three years in building my company I have spent hundreds of hours on the phone developing relationships. The one thing I've found is that when I shut up and listen, I'm likely to take one or two things away from the conversation that I wouldn't otherwise have known. Those things can end up propelling my business further, faster. The reality is you and I don't have thousands of dollars and thousands of hours to experiment, so it's important that you take time and learn what you can from other people so you don't have to pay for the same mistake, setback, or failure someone else has already experienced.

Offer to Help. After every single conversation I have I will end with the same couple sentences. First I call them by their name because people are programmed to respond to that. In this example, let's use Joe. "Joe, before I let you go, is there any value that I can add to you and your business even if it's as simple as making an introduction?" This question leaves the door open and lets Joe know that you sincerely care about him and his business. It also lets Joe know that you are acknowledging him and are offering to help him. This question is often answered with something like "Oh, most people don't ask that.", or "Yes, actually there is…." This is also the key to finding out their needs. Finally, I leave the conversation with "Great. If there is ever anything else I can do, please don't hesitate to reach out and let me know. Let's stay connected more often. You have my personal cell number so lock it in, and I have yours so I'll do the same. Take care and talk soon!" Since I left the caller with this statement, they now know I'm interested in furthering the relationship and I am going to follow up with them.

Follow Up. If you promised to make an introduction, then do so, and do it immediately. If you promised to send the individual your book, brochure, links to website, or anything else then do so, and do it immediately. When you do so, immediately you are building credibility with the individual and letting them know that they can trust you are going to do what you said. As you begin building these relationships, it's important to recognize that the more value you give, the more value you will receive in return. This is how the world's most successful leaders built their brand, reputation, and credibility, and it's how you too can do the same.

I love the power of social media and if it's utilized properly it can become one of your greatest assets in building relationships with some of the most successful individuals in the world. Just having thousands of contacts isn't enough. If you don't interact, engage, connect, speak with, and offer value to these connections then there is no point in having them at all.

Like I mentioned before, relationships are the foundation of success, and without them you won't get very far. I encourage you to look at your own platforms and start burning bridges with those that don't serve you and adding value to those that will serve you. Once you understand the power in relationships, nothing else will matter. Remember, this journey wasn't meant for you to take on your own.

LESSON 4: TELL STORIES

~~~

They Are The Most Powerful Gift You Can Share With Someone

Have you ever noticed how when you tell a story the audience becomes that much more attentive and interested in what you have to say? Storytelling is an art and one that not very many people are skilled at. Being a witness is what draws people closer, what grabs people's attention, and what compels people to take action. All of the stories I've shared throughout this book are raw, real, and relatable because I understand the power of being a witness. In today's fast paced technology driven world people aren't interested in facts as much as they are in stories that demonstrate facts and teach them how they can do it to.

Telling someone how to do something is not the same as showing them that it can be done. You've seen and will continue to see throughout this book that I love telling stories. I love sharing my life with you. I love demonstrating the value of the lessons I've been able to learn. Stories sell because they are easy to remember and even easier to tell.

Of all of the books you've read, events you've attended, and people you've talked with, usually the ones who tell stories are the ones you listen to and the ones you recommend. How do I know? Well, after releasing my first book a client of mine (Andrew Carlson) was asked during a radio interview if there was only one book in the world he would recommend what would it be? His response *"Be Ballsy! How Not To Suck At Love, Success, & Happiness."* When I asked why he chose my book, this was his exact response: "Because it was different. Every other book wasn't as personal as yours and that's why it resonated with me so well. Authenticity and being genuine are two main traits I look for in everyone. Plus it made me laugh and I love stories. Tony Robbins and Dr. Wayne Dyer are great but I wasn't as captivated by their books as much as I was with yours." In fact, Andrew, like many people have read *Be Ballsy!* cover to cover in one sitting and have recommended it to hundreds of other readers. Some of my readers have also told me they carry it around, because it's a great conversation piece.

I share this with you, because my books aren't written to be consumed as knowledge, set to the side to collect dust, and never be opened again. I've designed them to share with you my life, my knowledge, and the circumstances I was under and how I used these exact traits to turn my mess into my message. If I wasn't as confident as I am in my ability to deliver results, I wouldn't be as transparent as I am about what it takes to create that confidence and build those beliefs to get those results.

Stories work in two ways though. They can be positive or negative. Many of you reading this are probably in the same situation I was. Struggling, in debt, looking for customers, and wondering how you are going to make it to tomorrow or pay your next bill. But listen to me very carefully, because it is the stories that you are currently telling yourself that are keeping you from reaching the level of success you desire, being in the relationship you want, or even creating the level of happiness you deserve. I could've used every single one of the stories that I'm sharing with you to keep me from doing something with my life. I could've stayed stuck. I could've given up. I could've kept making the same mistakes, taking the same actions, and telling myself the same stories and drove myself into a suicidal depression. But I chose not to. I now choose to leverage all of the things that I've gone through to help others, most importantly to help you.

Stories are far more powerful than we realize. Stories can do one of two things: keep us stuck or motivate us to keep going. As you go throughout your day, recognize all of the stories you keep telling yourself. Maybe they're stories about how you aren't good enough, smart enough, pretty enough, or educated enough. Maybe you don't have the right relationships or enough money. Maybe you aren't in the perfect place, or have the perfect circumstances. I didn't either, but telling yourself that story is only going to keep you stuck. Stuck on the ferris wheel that keeps spinning round and round with no way off. Stop with the stories. Step into your fear. Turn your mess into your message and watch how your life transforms as a result.

LESSON 5: COMMUNICATE

~~~

It's The Only Way To Effectively Lead Teams, & Organizations

It's amazing how often we overlook communication as the root of our problem(s). I've worked in high level organizations and led teams of hundreds of employees in top Fortune 500 companies for five years and while there's often a tendency to play the blame game when something goes wrong. The truth is, it often comes down to the way we communicate with our colleagues. Take for example Rick. Rick was an amazing mentor to me and helped me climb up the chain of command very quickly. He was an aggressive, straight forward, open, honest man, who worked his ass off. While it was obvious to everyone that he would spend hours, and hours, in fact days and nights working, not everyone liked him.

Now I know what you're thinking, and of course I was thinking it too. What does that have to do with anything much less the effectiveness of the organization? Rick was a Co-Manager for Wal-Mart. He has three kids and a wife he left behind so he could travel with the organization, work his way up the ladder, and eventually go home to his family. Rick is also Asian. While in most parts of the world, that wouldn't matter, but in the store he managed in a small town in the NE corner of Iowa it did. You see, people didn't respect him, didn't listen to him, and didn't want anything to do with him. They would talk behind his back about how he chose to run the store. While they cared less about the impact the decisions he was making were having on the morale and the efficiency of the store itself.

In my opinion, Rick was an amazing man and we became close friends. In fact, so close we would travel store to store together. Rick and I would communicate on a daily basis but his inability to connect with my other colleagues was leaving him feeling drained and them feeling like he didn't care. He did care but he wasn't showing it in a way that people could understand, much less appreciate.

This happens inside the greatest organizations in the world on a daily basis. Managers care for their employees but they lack the communication skills and techniques to effectively communicate their feelings across the organization leaving both the managers and employees excited to be coming to work while leaving with more energy and fulfillment then when they came.

Communication is everything in today's technology driven, fast paced world. I love technology but I love people more. The only way to effectively communicate in an organization is to know, understand, and respect the people with whom you work.

Let's dig into each of these a little further so you get a true understanding of what I mean and how communication affects every aspect of the organization.

Know Your People. People are the backbone of your business. If you don't take the opportunity to introduce yourself, joke around, have fun, and work side by side with your employees, you are losing money. The more you have to hire people the more money it's costing your organization. A great example is Tony Hsieh, CEO of Zappos. Tony understands the dynamics of his organization and knows his people so well that he is able to maximize not only his employees' potential but the impact of the brand as a result.

Just showing up for work isn't enough. Just doing the work you're assigned isn't enough. Just closing the sale one time without getting a lifetime customer isn't enough. And it certainly isn't enough to show up to work and throw out the demands for the day without actually taking the time to get to know your frontline employees who are providing your end customers with the experience that has and continues to increase your organization's level of influence and success daily. It just isn't enough. So don't expect it to be!

Understand Your People. These people in your organization have families, personal lives, medical problems, and other priorities outside of work. When you understand the driving force, the reason why they show up each day, you not only become a better leader but they become a better employee. All of the highly successful and influential entrepreneurs and organizations I've worked with throughout the past decade with the happiest people, (managers and employees alike) who stay with their companies the longest, work in organizations that not only recognize but respect the need to have flexibility. While they don't allow people to take advantage of it, flexible working hours allows for the employee to prioritize what's most important in their life.

Respect Your People No adult likes being treated like a child. No one wants to be scolded, or put down for the work they did especially if the work isn't 100%. There are respectful ways to deal with situations like this without throwing your employees under the bus or making them feel like shit! The greatest leaders in the world are the ones who respect their employees, guide their employees, and share with their employees' ways to improve. There are dozens of ways respect positively impacts your organization, in fact far too many to list here.

Most importantly **Communicate With Your People.** Communication really is the key to success regardless of your title, role, or position. As a coach, I emphasize the importance of communication because if you can't communicate with your employees, then don't expect your customers to be happy or get results. I work closely with both my team and clients and oversee all aspects of my organization. In order to maximize your employees, and customers' potential as well as your bottom line, you MUST learn to listen, appreciate, and communicate in a way that gets people to buy into your vision, take action, and get excited about showing up each day. You see for Gen Y, a job is no longer just a job. It's a way for them to impact, influence, and inspire others to step into their greatness while they continue to do the same.

If Rick had done each of these three things, the impact he would've made and the buy-in from the employees he was managing would've been much higher and he would've been much happier. Let this be a lesson for you that no matter how well you think you're communicating, you can always improve.

LESSON 6: READ

~~~

There's Magic In The Pages Of A Book

No matter how busy you are, or how many "things" you have to get done reading is one of the greatest ways to expand your vocabulary, and increase your skillset. It isn't about how many books you can read, rather what principles those books teach you that you can actually apply to your life and your business. I know this lady who has more than 1,500 books on personal growth and development, and yet she doesn't have the love, success, and happiness she desires. She's spent years attending workshops, seminars, teleconferences, webinars, you name it she's probably attended it. Yet in searching for the answer to her "problems" she's failed to look within herself and recognize the only problem she has is herself.

Zig Ziegler once said "Your life will remain the same except for the people you meet and the books you read." While I love Zig, this is only true if you apply the principles, strategies, disciplines, and habits being taught throughout the pages of the books you read and the people you surround yourself with. You've probably also heard, "You are the average sum of the five people you hang out with." This too is BS. If you sit around a table with millionaires that isn't going to make you a millionaire unless you take action. If you sit around a table with broke people that isn't going to make you a broke person unless you stop taking action. In this quote, what the author is referencing is the fact that you must be constantly increasing your skill level, expanding your mindset, and taking action.

I've read hundreds of books. In fact I've spent the last three years of my life obsessed with personal growth. I love reading, learning, writing, speaking, and coaching but I promise I wouldn't be able to get my clients the results they've been able to get without actually investing the time and testing the waters myself. My library is filled with books from Jim Rohn, Dani Johnson, Dr. Phil, Deepak Chopra, Barbara Johnson, and hundreds of others. I've been known to read up to five books a week. Consuming information without applying information though is a disaster. While it's critical to your success to read, it's more important to apply the information in a way that works best for you and your business. Utilize and capitalize off of the information that is applicable to you and dump the rest.

You see for thousands of years people want to give advice on love, success, and happiness and yet they are miserable, ill equipped, and only doing so based on desires but not actual results. I believe being an author is a privilege and one that I take very seriously, because I wouldn't give any advice that I haven't applied myself. Reading is a journey into the depths of your soul. It's a visual experience unlike any other. Reading is one of the most powerful things you can do for yourself. It will inspire, captivate, and motivate you to take action. If it wasn't for my obsession with reading, learning, growing, and expanding, I certainly would not be writing this book nor giving my clients or you advice on how they can have it all, all at the same time.

Reading has been and continues to be one of my daily disciplines. Regardless of how many pages I can consume in the time I pick up the book, reading is a way to calm the body and clear the mind. It's a way to take your attention off of all of the things you need to do. What I've found with many of the people I've been able to help, is that they are overwhelmed, discontent, and ready to increase their results in life and yet they participate in the very activities that take away from accelerating their learning and ability to grow such as watching TV, or listening and reading the news. Reading is a simple, small, and free thing you can do to tremendously accelerate your growth and one of the quickest, easiest, and most effective ways regardless of your title, occupation, or industry to impact your own life and that of your organization.

I challenge you to head to your nearest bookstore or even Goodwill and pick up some great reads. Practice just reading 15 minutes a day and notice over a period of 27 months that you've read 47 books. That's far more then you are currently reading. Not only are you expanding your knowledge and growing but you are supporting a good cause to help mentally challenged people making it a win-win situation.

LESSON 7: JOURNAL

~~~

Pen To Paper Will Make Your Dreams Greater

Many people ask how I can write blog posts and do videos on such a regular basis. Or how I can write books back to back. The reality is that blogging is like journaling. It's a necessity to compile my thoughts and opinions while providing an opportunity for others to hear and respond to what I am thinking. While most people keep notebooks with years and years of thoughts, ideas, fears, hopes, and dreams, I express mine in a way that resonates and compels both myself and others to take action. In the dedication of this book I wrote "If I could dedicate a book to myself this would be the one. It's a simple reminder of all of the insanity one must endure to live beyond their wildest dreams." Writing for me is an expression of what I have and what I am going to accomplish while taking others along with me on the journey.

I feel like it's my duty, obligation, and responsibility to share with you my journey, struggles, heartaches, setbacks, and successes because this thing called life isn't meant to be lived alone and this journey of personal growth isn't meant to be a journey of one. You and I have both been blessed with unique talents, gifts, and abilities. While I know and understand most people aren't willing to share their life and aren't as open or transparent about their business as I am, I also know that it benefits far more people then I realize. And, far more people than I could ever impact through individual conversations.

Recently I was having a conversation with a close friend. He was telling me he was "jealous of me" and then we continued talking about the gift of gab and being able to put pen to paper and just write. I have been blessed but that has nothing to do with it, because everyone has been blessed in different ways. I've taken my blessing and started tapping into my potential, so I can make a big difference and add value to others life which is much more important than just being blessed. You don't have to do what I do. But, I want to share with you three reasons you should.

Track Goals. Blogging, journaling, and writing books is not only a great way to track goals, but it's also a great way to monitor them. One of my favorite things to do on a regular basis is to take out a sheet of paper and write down all of the things I'm working towards during the month. This not only allows me to have a clear direction in where I'm going but it also becomes my reason why. Writing down these goals acts like my vision board, except I believe it's much more powerful. You see a vision board is something you look at from time to time but you don't carry around. Writing down a list of things you want on a simple piece of paper and carrying that around with you is a profound reminder that every action you take must lead you to getting what it is that you truly desire. The more you look at the paper, the more you're reminded of what you want, and the more action you will take. The more action you take, the more motivated you become and the more you get accomplished. This is one of the simplest, easiest, and most effective ways I've found to help me not only get more done in less time but to truly stay focused on and reach my end goals.

Capture Lessons. The lessons that are captured in my books are more important than the words I'm putting on paper. Lessons teach people what to do and how to do it while shortening the learning curve and saving thousands and sometimes millions of dollars in the process. Even if I don't have the opportunity to work with you one-on-one, I believe that it's important to share with you the exact steps I took, the exact blueprint I followed, and the exact mistakes I made. If something in the pages of this book helps you, then writing it was well worth my investment because there is no point in two of us paying for the same mistake.

Leave A Legacy. I was asked how I was able to write my first book *Be Ballsy! How Not To Suck At Love, Success & Happiness* in under 30 days, and why I choose to write it when I did. Most people know I don't have the greatest memory, so the quickest way to remember details is to get them down on paper. But, why just get them down on paper, why not share them with the world as well? I'm building my company so I can leave a legacy, make an impact, and create a difference for centuries to come. While I intend to impact as many people as I can with my time here on earth, I would rather work hard and sacrifice now so my children, grandchildren, great grandchildren, and others know that attaining any level of love, success, and happiness doesn't come easy. But, more importantly, they can read exactly what I was thinking, when I was thinking it.

How many of us have truly sat down and had a conversation with our parents and grandparents and know what they did as kids, what their passions were, what their struggles were, what their successes were, and have the ability to know what they were thinking at the exact moment they were thinking it? Not many. In fact while I do know many things about my parents, many of the stories they share are the same stories told on a different day. Journaling, blogging, and writing books allows future generations to look back and understand where I came from, what I went through, and what I was thinking, So my story and impact lives beyond my life span.

I challenge you to start writing down your thoughts, ideas, hopes, dreams, struggles, plans, and successes. I challenge you to spend the next 30 days writing something. Don't tell me you have nothing to write. If you aren't a good writer or it doesn't come easy, then simply grab a voice recorder and speak your thoughts and create an MP3. You may not see the significance of doing this now or in your lifetime. It may not impact the world, but it will impact your family and generations of your family to come. It's time well spent. Let me give you an example of how powerful writing can be, because I've written well over 300 blogs and magazine articles for major publications in the last 3 years and now I'm finishing my second book in less than 56 days.

I went home to visit my parents and sat my first book *Be Ballsy!* along with my laptop on the coffee table in the living room and took off to do something else. Less than 10 minutes later I walk in and see my mom reading this book. Astonished because she absolutely never, and I mean NEVER reads books, I asked her what she was doing. She looks up and says "I've learned more about you from this book then you've told me. You didn't tell me you were in love!" Well I didn't think I needed too.

At that point she was only on page 9. You see, I'm not only writing these books for myself but for my family and their families. Am I proud that I've been blessed with the unique ability to write and tell stories? Absolutely. People for centuries have provided the same content I am, but I'm presenting and packaging it in a way that is raw, real, and relatable. That's where the power lies. The principles and techniques I'm sharing with you aren't new. In fact they've worked for thousands of years in thousands of companies. None of this will apply or work if you don't use it, so take a couple minutes a day and write down your setbacks and successes and share these powerful tools and stories with others to help them along the way.

LESSON 8: MEDITATE

~~~

It's The Easiest Way To Create Peace Of Mind

Most people ask about the significance and how I came up with the name of my company Briella Arion. I meditate daily and one day the name kept playing and replaying in my head. I looked up the meaning and it not only made sense but it stuck. Throughout my time of difficulties the meaning had significance and that still rings true today. Briella is female and means "God is my strength" and Arion is male and means "enchantment or melodious". Meditation is a powerful way to relax both the mind and the body.

One of my employees and I were recently having a discussion surrounding the power of meditation and its impact. There are many ways for an individual to meditate and there are many programs on meditation. Whether you meditate to music or meditate on your own, it's a great way to get clarity surrounding your goals and create peace of mind.

Meditation, while powerful, can also be negative. I've seen people take it way too far and end up living like monks for a couple years until they realize the way they practiced meditation wasn't the way it's designed to be used. Like many other things, meditation is a tool, and a powerful one if used properly. I've been meditating daily for nearly three years now and I spend no more than 10-15 minutes right before I go to bed clearing my mind. Meditation is like a cleanse, it gets rid of negative and toxic thoughts. The exact thoughts that are keeping you where you currently are.

Some of you may be questioning what meditation is and why I would recommend integrating it into your life. The easiest way for me to explain meditation is like this: If you're a woman and ever noticed your man sitting on the couch completely zoned out and you've asked him something like "Honey, what are you thinking about?" and his reply is "Nothing." Yet you continue to nag at him and say, "You can't possibly be thinking about nothing. Really. What are you thinking about?" So he comes up with some bullshit just to get you off his back and make you think he was thinking about something when he really wasn't. That's a form of meditation. Meditation is thinking about nothing.

Meditation is very simple. If you haven't practiced it, I highly encourage you to do so and notice the results you get as you make it part of your daily disciplines. The process of meditation is no doubt vague and hard to understand. I remember my first time meditating like it was yesterday. I had just finished a yoga class at a local gym. The instructor turned on this transcendental music and I laid flat on my back, arms to my sides, motionless as I fell deeper and deeper into a trance. The music was very soothing and calming much like you would play for a baby to get them to sleep. The sounds of this music affect and restructure the brain waves. These movements throughout time with the continued practice of meditation create many positive effects in our lives and business. Meditation helps us focus better, have less anxiety, more creativity, compassion and less stress. Who isn't looking for those things? Meditation also slows down the aging process and the best part is it's free! If you haven't tried it, do so. You won't regret it.

LESSON 9: BE VULNERABLE

~~~

The Story Of How Matt & I Met

I have a confession. Being vulnerable isn't easy. In fact, it's one of the hardest things you can do. At least for me that is, and I assume that since you are reading this, it probably is true for you too. I remember driving to Chicago with a rental car hoping that my life would somehow change, thinking that this trip would enhance my business. I was hoping that this trip would make me more money, close more clients, and dramatically increase my bottom line.

When I drove to Chicago, I didn't have a plan. I didn't have a ton of money either. What I did have though was hope and a dream to make my business better. I remember meeting Matthew Lee, (an 8x best-selling author with Jack Canfield) who is now my coach. I had no money for a coach, no reason to have a coach, and didn't actually understand how bad I truly needed a coach.

I created a FB status that said, "I'm going to be in Chicago. I've cleared my schedule for the week, so if you want to meet up, please reach out and let me know. I can meet you anywhere." At 8 p.m. I arrive at Starbucks in I guess what's considered to be the safe side of south Chicago. I meet Matt, a 6 ft. 7' tall basketball player. We conversed for hours and as he's explaining to me his background, story, and successes, I remember thinking I wish I could figure out how he had come this far in such a short period of time. I left Chicago with plenty of new personal connections, but it didn't change my life and it certainly didn't change my business.

The next time I was in Chicago, I asked Matt if we could meet up and go over a deal I was doing with a client. That's when I found myself sitting across the table scared, nervous, insecure, and completely out of my comfort zone. Matt was asking me hard questions, deep questions. He was asking me to step into my full potential. He asked me to commit to myself that I was willing to do whatever it takes, no matter what it took to live the life I desired. He wanted me to hire him as my coach.

As I'm sitting there and he's hitting every pain point imaginable, he says, "Are you in or are you out?" I'm aggressive, powerful, and a fighter and there was no way I was sitting out, no way I was giving up, and no way I wasn't going to do whatever it took. So, he continued with; "How much money is in your bank account?" Laughing because I didn't want to tell him, and nervous that he would judge me if he found out I tried avoiding the question. Which not only didn't work, but made Matt probe even deeper. He was now demanding, aggressive, yet authentic, genuine, loving, caring and compassionate.

That's when I had only one of two choices to call it quits or to buck up and commit. After telling him I only had $200, he asked if I could PayPal him $50. Now, I didn't really have $50. I was days away from having to return a rental car I couldn't afford. I was broke but willing, insecure but tough, most importantly I was vulnerable. I went out to my car grabbed a $100 bill asked the cashier to split it and threw the money on the table. Matt wasn't impressed and he shouldn't have been. $50 is a joke, and no one should be willing to work for that. Especially a high level coach and someone as successful as Matt. But he wasn't willing to give up and neither was I. In fact he has been, and continues to be, a huge asset to my company.

I finally let my guard down. I finally stepped up and committed to making my business work. I finally had someone that believed in me enough to coach me for $50 upfront and 20% of whatever I made. I felt the pressure release. I felt free. I no longer felt like I was alone. In fact, I felt compelled to take more action since I had money on the table. More action then I have ever taken before.

The lesson: no matter how insecure, uncomfortable or worried you are, there are others who have been through what you are experiencing. There are leaders who are willing to guide you along the way, and show you the shortcuts to lessons they spent years learning, and thousands of dollars investing in. You are never too good enough to ask for help. Be brave, be vulnerable, and most importantly, be you. Don't worry what other people think, because they probably aren't thinking that at all.

LESSON 10: ASK FOR HELP

~~~

Life Is A Game But It's Not Meant To Be Played Alone

One of the lessons Matt reminds me about on a regular basis is that asking for help doesn't make you weaker it actually makes you stronger. One of my weaknesses is asking for help. I would rather figure it out on my own, reinvent the wheel, or learn the hard way, then ask for help. I've learned over time that's one of the longest, hardest, and most ineffective ways to accomplish anything. I'm not paying Matt to take it easy, hold my hand, and be a shoulder for me to cry on. I hired Matt to be tough, real, and call me out on my BS. If you have a personality like mine, then not a lot of people are willing to stand up and call it like it is, because people are often intimidated by titles, accolades, and strong personalities.

In this crazy, busy world it doesn't matter what title you have, or how much success you've attained. You didn't get there by yourself. For those of you who like to claim you are "self-made", let me just be brutally honest. That's the biggest load of bullshit I've ever heard. I know you woke up early, stayed up late, and worked your ass off, but I also know you had help along the way. For anyone who claims to be "self-made", or believes in being "self-made", I can almost guarantee you aren't going to like what I have to say next, but I do encourage you to keep reading. We've all had to fall on our faces a couple times, get back up, and try again. In order to not make the same mistake again, we've had to ask for help. We were required to make or find a way.

Asking for help is one of the hardest lessons I've ever learned, and yet one of the most valuable. Asking for help is a strong indicator that you are willing to set your ego aside and seek the advice that can propel your business or life further than you ever could alone. I've had to ask for help many times. Just recently, I was trying to figure out how I'm going to create a sales funnel that converts. This sales funnel also needed to attract the clients I was interested in serving and repel the clients I wasn't interested in serving. Like many times, I was conversing via FB and I happened to be speaking with the guy who built John Assaraf's sales funnel. Now that wouldn't be a big deal if John wasn't a big deal.

First and most importantly, I began building a relationship with this guy. As time progressed, he offered insight into my sales funnel, provided ideas, helped create sales copy, and wanted to do a one minute video for me valued at $17,500 for free. These are the kind of opportunities you are only offered once, and only offered because you aren't afraid of being honest, getting hurt, or being rejected. I could have told him I have the best sales funnel in the world, it converts high, it brings in qualified leads that I'm able to close regularly and everything is perfect. But that would've been the furthest thing from the truth.

What happened was we built a great relationship. We both added value to one another's businesses. He asked me to help him change certain disciplines and habits I have experience dealing with while he helped develop a bad ass sales funnel. The point is you are not an island, you are not made to go through this life alone. You were born for greatness, born to tap into your full potential, and born to be all that you can be. That requires asking for help. That requires getting out of your own way so that you can move quicker, easier, and more effectively towards achieving your goals, hopes, and dreams. Asking for help is one of the smallest things you can do that will bring you a big return.

LESSON 11: GET A COACH

~~~

Knowing How To Qualify A Coach Is Just As Important As Having One

A lot of people waver about or are unsure of getting a coach. Getting a coach is a significant asset to both you and your company. But, it will only be an asset if you are open to listening, taking action, and implementing the strategies, habits, and disciplines needed to achieve the goals you've set out for yourself. I've had my own personal coach for nearly a year. In addition to having him as my go-to guy, I've added additional support such as fitness experts, voice experts, sales funnel experts, among various other experts. While one can coach on the various aspects of business, they will never be a master in all of those areas. Matt does a great job helping me create well thought out execution plans, and helping me stay accountable. However, he isn't focused on vocal exercises, or physical exercises, or anything outside of the scope of his expertise.

I was having a conversation the other day with an entrepreneur from Silicon Valley, California, who has hired coaches before, has regrets about his lack of success or rather limited belief that he lacks success, and his inability to resonate with, or see value in coaching because he's invested and been burned one too many times. Now, while I wouldn't take him on as a client, I wanted to include this as a lesson because he asked a question that needs to be answered by someone who not only has results, but can prove their results. His question was, "How do you know a good coach from a bad one?"

The reality is that there are thousands of coaches and not every coach is going to be right fit for you. With the coaching industry growing at an incredibly rapid pace, and people using the term coach inappropriately to create an income stream without care and concern for their clients, it can be tough to find someone who is truly in it for YOU and not for themselves.

Here are some distinct characteristics that separate the real from the want-to-be coach.

REAL COACHES:

Sell VALUE vs. TIME.

One of the first things I tell my clients is we will meet as much as you need me, but as little as possible. Coaching is all about serving the client, reaching the client's goals, providing direction, accountability, and clarity for the client. Let's use an analogy here we can all relate to. Suppose you are going to the dentist because you are in a lot of pain from a tooth that you know needs to be pulled. You don't care where the dentist got his degree from, how many times he's done this before, if his nurses are certified, how many patients he's helped, and who those patients are. What you truly care about is getting rid of the pain. After all, that's the whole reason you are there.

The same is true for coaching. People seek out coaches because they are in pain, they've made a decision to seek professional guidance, and they want to see results as quickly, effortlessly, and painlessly as possible. So let's say you're an average person who works really hard for their money and you ask the dentist "How much is this going to cost?" The dentist says "$600." And, you're thinking that's a whole weeks' worth of work, so you proceed to ask, "How long is this going to take?" The dentist quickly replies "5 minutes but it can take as long as you want the price is still going to be the same." You are there because of severe pain. No amount of medication is going to resolve the issue so the only option is to pay a premium price to a service provider that can solve your problem in less than 5 minutes getting you in, out, and on your way back to a normal routine, essentially saving you both time and money. This principle is also true for a professional coach, they charge premium prices, working with limited clients, delivering massive results, as quickly, effortlessly, and painlessly as possible.

Real Coaches Qualify Their Clients.

Using the same analogy, let's say you went to the dentist because every time you flossed, your gums would bleed, essentially meaning you have a gum disease. And, while the dentist could fix this he realizes that there are specialists out there who are more qualified, and more expensive, but have the tools, knowledge, and resources necessary to fix the problem immediately. They are called specialists because they specialize and focus solely on one thing. So he sends you to a Periodontist, or if you need braces he would send you to an Orthodontist.

The same is true for coaching. If the coach you are speaking with isn't qualifying their clients, then they aren't maximizing their own potential, their businesses potential or the potential of their clients. I turn away far more clients then I help, because they don't meet the qualifications required to become a client. The more specialized a person becomes, the higher their price, creating a premium product in the marketplace for only those who can truly afford and find value in the service. In any of these cases, if you use the excuse, "I don't have enough money.", you will be turned away. Don't get me wrong, there are plenty of coaches who don't qualify, and plenty of coaches who sell time, but those are the same coaches who AREN'T truly dedicated to not only your success but their own. These are the same coaches that also refuse to walk the talk.

Real Coaches Have No Agenda.

Traditional coaching is like a therapy session, where you sit down, list your problems, hope the person you are telling has an idea or response, and can get you results. Those days have come and gone. Non-traditional coaching for people who truly want results has no agenda, and if there was an agenda the only thing on it would say "Get Results." In a fast pace, information overwhelm, instant access, tech driven world, we are easily distracted thousands of times a day. This causes our dreams, goals, and ambitions to quickly and easily derail. When you find someone who not only has the results you desire, but can teach you how to implement the systems and disciplines necessary to achieve those exact results, you quickly realize that you can work less and get paid more. Serving the right clients who become happier, healthier and wealthier creating an endless stream of referrals and repeat business. There isn't a coach on the planet that doesn't want to create these types of stories and results.

Real Coaches Genuinely Care & Are Incredibly Authentic.

Whoever it is that you decide to choose as your coach should prove that they genuinely have your best interest in mind and are there to focus on you and solve your problems. Coaches whose sole purpose is to fund their bank account and dreams have zero interest in actually putting in the time and doing the work it takes to help you achieve your goals. Look for coaches who walk the talk, who are incredibly authentic and real, and don't care whether or not you get offended by their words or actions because they are doing what's best for you as their client, while helping you get comfortable being uncomfortable, so you can get the results you want in the shortest, most effective way possible. As you can see, it's all about YOU!

Real Coaches Require a MASSIVE Commitment.

The coach who truly wants to help you tap into your full potential and maximize your business is going to ask you to make a MASSIVE commitment, and they aren't going to accept a commitment from you based on money alone. They are going to require that you are committed to results mentally, emotionally, physically, and psychologically. They are going to push buttons, make you uncomfortable, and create pain. This in turn helps you grow and ultimately this is going to dramatically transform both your life and lifestyle personally, professionally, and financially. That is the whole reason you wanted a hire a coach to begin with.

REAL COACHES know their value, believe in their value, and offer their value to the marketplace in a way that repels "want to be's" and attracts people who are truly committed at the highest levels to getting MASSIVE results. If you are considering working with a coach, use the criteria above to qualify and decide whether the person you are speaking with has your best interest in mind and can get you the results you desire. If you need help, have questions, or want to be pointed in the right direction, feel free to reach out, and remember price is never the issue when it comes to the cost of success.

Getting a coach is one of the best decisions, if not THE best decision you will ever make. I was speaking with a high six-figure entrepreneur the other day, and there were certain things in his business that he wanted. These included: more media attention, to double his income, to qualify and close corporate clients sooner. So I asked him a simple question. "Do you have a coach?" His response was, "No, I go to a lot of events. I'm involved in some masterminds. I listen to audios, read books, and go to seminars/webinars. I've worked on marketing campaigns for Nike, Tiffany, Eastern Bank Limited, Reebok, and Chevron, among various others." Letting him continue to speak for a minute, I countered that with, "Then you know the best investment you can make is the investment in yourself." He, of course still hesitant because he's rarely on the other side of the table, pitches to potential clients 13-14 times a week, has a successful business, invests highly in personal growth, and is doing really well says, "Ok, no one's ever pitched me on coaching. I get pitched daily for lots of things but not coaching. I meet coaches at events at least once a week, and last week I met one who tried to pitch me but backed down." And, so as I continued to listen to what he was saying, and continued to take notes about what he wanted, I took the opportunity to pitch him and he became a really high paying client. This is important for several reasons:

- No one is too successful to have a coach.
- Value is an exchange for money, and there is no reason to back down on what you know you are able to deliver. No matter how intimidating someone might seem.
- Confidence is irreplaceable.
- You can't get to where you are going without accountability, clarity, and a roadmap.
- It costs money to stay where you are, and it costs more money to go back to where you've been.

LESSON 12: INVEST

~~~

Greater Investments Bring Greater Returns

Those people who have it all, all at the same time, have made significant investments in things that have brought a significant return. This is one of my favorite lessons because I believe that investing is one of the greatest things you can do for yourself and your bank account. In every conversation I've had with wealthy people, there are three investments that they will undoubtedly make on a consistent basis to build their portfolio and wealth. These three investments bring higher returns than anything you could possibly purchase.

They Invest In Relationships. Like I've said many, many times throughout this book. Relationships are everything. They always were, and always will be. Investing in relationships costs nothing but your time, and there isn't an investment with a higher return than that of a relationship. Wealthy individuals are constantly connecting, communicating, networking, and engaging in conversation regardless of where they are.

They Invest In Real Estate. When I say invest in real estate, I don't mean buy foreclosed homes, or flip properties. The best investment in real estate is multiple family properties. The additional stream of income these properties make is worth the investment in and of itself. When you add on the increased property value with a few small upgrades, the return on your invest also increases. I'm not by any means telling you I'm a real estate expert, because I'm not. From the conversations I've had, and research I've done, this is hands down the #1 investment real estate professionals and multi-property real estate investors invest in. Multi-Family properties make great assets, because it's a less competitive, yet a far more lucrative, market. Most people don't have money to throw at roofing repairs for three individual properties, but recovering one roof that brings in three incomes makes the investment more efficient and profitable. It's not only a great investment for the beginner, but it's also great for the seasoned investor.

They Invest In Themselves. This is the single greatest investment you can ever make in your life. There is nothing that compares or comes close to comparing the return that you will receive from investing in yourself. I've personally invested thousands of dollars and thousands of hours in personal growth. I've read hundreds of books, listened to endless hours of audios, watched hours of YouTube videos, hired personal coaches, attended webinars, teleconferences, seminars, and private events. I've spent hours at the gym training, in the kitchen prepping, and spent days planning but...

Don't Let Your Ego Stand In The Way Of Your Success!

If I knew in the beginning what I know now, I would have put skin in the game a hell of a lot sooner. I would've hired a coach so much earlier. I would've stopped telling bullshit stories to myself about how awesome I am, and how I have everything I need to do it on my own. I would've given up what little money I had so I could have more money, because there is no greater feeling in the world then doing what you love and getting paid what you're worth. Many coaches, professionals, and executives think they have their life figured out, their business under control, and their investments creating great returns. Reality is, when it truly comes down to it, the best investment you can make is the investment in yourself.

Hiring a coach has been the most rewarding, fulfilling, revenue and confidence boosting investment I have ever made. Regardless of the cost, time, effort, energy, and money I spend, I am all in. Not just all in financially, but all in mentally, physically, emotionally, and psychologically as well. I am much happier, healthier, and wealthier than I've ever been. While I would love to say it's possible to do it on your own, it's not. Give up the power play and remove the ego and all you have left standing between you and success is the story you keep telling yourself and letting yourself believe. I want to leave you with this thought: When it comes to playing the game you are either all in OR not in at all.

Beyond these three things, there are many other things that you can invest in and I encourage you to invest in. But this book was written and designed to give you the simplest, easiest, and most effective tips, tools, and knowledge so you can live a life beyond your wildest dreams. These three things alone will help you do just that.

LESSON 13: FAITH

~~~

You Either Have It Or You Don't

Is your prayer like a steering wheel or a spare tire? A steering wheel guides you in the right direction. A spare tire you don't worry or care about until you break down and need it. I'm not into organized religion, but I don't think you can live without faith. Faith is a strong belief in something other than yourself. While I'm not going to use this lesson to provide endless Bible verses and sermons on getting to know Jesus. I am going to use this lesson to help you recognize the importance of faith and its impact on your business.

And, if you're a person who believes in science or something else, skip this lesson. It isn't going to hurt my feelings. You don't have to answer to me, and I completely respect your beliefs. It's not my place to judge or condemn you for what you do or do not believe. If you do believe in faith, and I truly hope you do, then read on my friend, because this lesson is sure to help you.

Faith requires action. I know that every seed I plant will bear fruit if I keep planting seeds and nurturing them. They will never bear fruit without time and attention though. Much like a farmer plows the land, plants the seed, let's nature nurture them for the season and harvests the crop, faith requires action. Like Martin Luther King once said, "Faith is taking the first step without seeing the whole staircase."

I didn't know what the hell I was doing when I first got into business. I didn't know how to find clients, create products, close sales, or package, much less position, myself to get results. I aimlessly planted seeds, but I still planted them nonetheless. These weren't seeds of fear or doubt, but seeds of faith without knowing what the outcome or result was going to be. Every day I would wake up and take action. Even if it was the smallest of actions, I knew it would pay off and it has. You don't have to know where you are going to end up. Oftentimes you won't. But you do have to take consistent action and believe that you are going to be rewarded with enough patience and time.

Faith Makes The Impossible Possible. I can honestly say I thought I knew what love was. There is nothing that compares to the happiness and love I receive from my significant other, Rohan. He's the most amazing friend and companion anyone could ever ask for. I was ok being single, but I still believed that someday I would find the one. I just didn't know when, how or with who. That's what faith is. Faith is believing that it's possible and yet not knowing. I knew that I would have a successful company, and build a successful brand, but I didn't know how long it would take, who I would meet along the way, or how it would happen. I only knew that it would. I'm sure you believe that a breakthrough will happen for you. With a little time and a lot of faith it will.

Fear Is Faith. I don't know that our relationship will last forever, but I have faith it will. I don't know if this business will be around for decades, but I have faith it will. I don't know a lot of things, but my faith is bigger than my fears. Fear is faith. Faith that it won't work out.

Faith is believing in something beyond what currently exists for you. I'm a huge believer in God, study the Bible, and go to church weekly. That doesn't make what I believe in right or wrong. We all have our own values and beliefs and faith is high on my list. The lesson here is to have a little faith, and your luck will automatically increase.

LESSON 14: HAVE HIGH INTEGRITY

~~~

Do What You Say You're Going To Do When You Say You're Going To Do It

The classic "I'm entitled" syndrome doesn't work when it comes to leadership. No matter how much money you make or what title you were given, when it comes to running a successful business or creating any success in your life, having integrity really does matter. I've been in the boardrooms of multi-million dollar organizations, and there hasn't been a single time to date that a CEO or member of the board has shown up late for a meeting or sales pitch. When you are committed to being somewhere or doing something, it's important that, unless you have a dire situation, you do the very things you say you're going to do, when you say you're going to do them.

Success will come and go, but integrity lasts forever. In fact, integrity is what builds or destroys your character. True leaders understand that it isn't about over promising and under delivering, but about under promising and over delivering. When it comes to sales and results, people want the quickest, easiest, most effective and profitable way possible, but sometimes a simple conversation surrounding their goals with a clear plan of action over a period of time is much more realistic than a promise built on a dream.

In job interviews, candidates tend to exaggerate on their current skills and abilities. In sales, salesman tend to over promise and under deliver in not only the quality, but the expectation of the product. In boardrooms, people tend to exaggerate on the quarter's goals and objectives. In organizations, employees call in sick because they want a day off, or don't have enough vacation time. CEO's overstate their projected earnings. In coaching/client relationships, clients say they want one thing, but end up wanting something completely different. From our childhood, we are taught that a little white lie isn't going to make a difference but when it comes to love, success, and happiness integrity makes all the difference.

Integrity is one of the most powerful traits a person can have. The other day, I was having a conversation with a television producer. As we are working on a project together now and going into the future, he asked if I would be willing to do a couple events with him where we promote each other and our passions. We discussed dates, times, and details. As we did, I told him I can't promise those specific dates will work so before I confirm let me check my calendar and get back with him. In less than 24 hours, I followed up to confirm the dates, times, and details to ensure that we were going to work together. Integrity isn't just about showing up. Integrity is doing what you say you are going to do, when you say you are going to do it. Then following up to make sure it's done.

I could have promised to be there, and not shown up. I could have promised to talk about one thing, and then talked about something completely different. The way you show up, the way you present yourself, and the way you respect yourself is the way you teach people how to treat you in return. When it comes to love, success, and happiness there are no short cuts, or easy ways out.

The value you have in trusting others, and the value people have in trusting you is beyond anything that can be measured. It's been said that customers will only do business with people they know, but that's not true. What is true is that people will only do business with those they trust. When it comes to doing a deal, especially a million dollar deal, there is nothing more important, not even the reputation of the company, then the integrity of the people doing the deal.

The definition of integrity that I live by, is you must be the same person you are in public as you are in your own home. Integrity is a moral, it's something I highly value. Let me give you an example of a person without integrity. A person I would never trust or do business with.

A once close friend of mine would dress up in very expensive apparel, and show up at the office with his feet placed on his desk. He would crunch the numbers, give the orders, spend the day answering the phone and emails, and let his employees deal with the clients. At home though, it was like he was a completely different person. As 33, he still couldn't afford to live on his own. He couldn't afford not to have more than one job. And, he certainly couldn't afford the Armani suits, Louis Vuitton belts, and other ridiculously expensive clothing he would buy just to show people at the office he was "made of money" when in fact we barely had any at all.

This is not integrity. Actually, I consider this stupidity. There is no reason to invest in things to make people believe that you can afford something that you can't. That you are someone that you aren't. That you care about something that you don't. Titles, positions, and salaries don't matter, because it isn't something people value as high as they value integrity. Money doesn't buy love. Money doesn't buy success. Money doesn't buy happiness. It only increases it. I'll leave this lesson with one of my favorite quotes from Will Smith "Too many people are buying things they can't afford, with money that they don't have... to impress people that they don't like!" Don't be one of them.

LESSON 15: BE AGGRESSIVE

~~~

Stay Hungry

When I say be aggressive, I don't mean be an asshole. You see, all too often we have "starving artists" syndrome. Meaning that we can't focus on anyone but ourselves, or anyone else's needs but our own. That mindset benefits no one. It especially doesn't benefit your bank account. Being aggressive is about knowing who you want to target, how you want to target them, and learning how to get them to say "yes" without the hassle.

If you're like me, then you hate aggressive sales people. They're pushy, nosey, and just plain rude. If I go into a store and a sales person runs up to me asking about this, that, and the other, or if I get put in a dressing room and they bring me piles of clothes I "might like", I will never shop there again. Or I'll just tell them to shut up and leave me alone...in my head. Seriously, I'm not that mean, but I'm not that nice either. I think there is a proper way to do sales, and being pushy, rude, and aggressive is one of the worst ways.

In business, if you expect any level of success it's important to focus on the factors that will get you the results you desire and aggressively take action towards them. For example, if you are looking to increase your bottom line, then you need to be aggressively finding people to have conversations with. If you want to get your product out to as many people as possible, then you need to be building relationships with people who have access to the market that you're looking to serve. If you want to build a new product, then you need to find someone who has already done something similar to what you want to do and have them guide you through the process. Aggressively taking the action you know you should be taking shouldn't occur when you want to take it, but when you need to take it. Don't expect for a minute to sit on your ass and get results. It isn't going to happen. Don't expect that your goals are going to jump of the paper and manifest themselves. It isn't going to happen. Don't expect that you are going to make one phone call and close a major deal. It isn't going to happen.

Success and money don't come that easy. It's amazing to me how many businesses have no idea who their target market is or how to reach that market. The ones that do know their market have complicated their message and marketing so much that they have reached the ceiling of complexity and that's stopped them from increasing both their market share and revenue. The key to breaking through this ceiling of complexity and knowing your target audience is understanding your #1 objective in business. A lot of people are hungry, so hungry in fact they're starving. Starving for a relationship. Starving for a successful business. Starving to keep food on the table and a roof over their head. Yet they aren't taking the action necessary to get the results they desire.

Being aggressive is simply about knowing what you want to achieve, and then taking whatever action you need to take to reach that goal. Let me give you an example. Lots of times people will come to me and talk about how ashamed they are that they haven't reached the level of success they desire, haven't found the relationship they want, or haven't made the money they need. Being afraid, ashamed, and insecure isn't going to get you anywhere. I call that digging your own grave. Step into that fear and your confidence will increase. As it does you will notice that voice in your head and the people surrounding you becoming quieter and start asking questions with intrigue. Instead of being ashamed, be proud. Instead of choosing to be mediocre, average, and content with your life, choose to do something about it. Choose to take action. Instead of being insecure, be brave and step out in the world. Anyone who's successful at any level has had to be brave at one point or another in their journey.

When you aggressively go in the direction you desire, shame, doubt, fear, and insecurities become less and less. People start asking questions and noticing that you are no longer one of them. You are no longer spending hours in front of the television listening to the news. You no longer binge on junk food. You no longer make excuses about why you can't work out. Instead they ask questions like, "Why are you reading?", "What are you reading?", "Why are going to those events?", "What are you getting out of those events?", "Why are you working on the weekends and late into the evenings?", "Why?", "Why?", "Why?". And yet, that doesn't inspire them to get off their ass and do anything until several years later. In some cases earlier they notice that you've lost weight, are making a significant amount of money, live in your dream home, have a great relationship, and are happier than you've ever been, and so on. The point is that all of the small actions when done on a consistent and aggressive basis, have huge payoffs.

When my family, friends, and community told me I couldn't do it, I didn't acknowledge them. I simply let it be, and started taking aggressive action. When they noticed I wasn't attending social functions and refused to engage in the same activities they were, they questioned why. I didn't answer. I simply continued to take more action. When business people called me crazy, I didn't let that bother me. I simply took more action. There is no point in fighting or dealing with people who aren't willing to do what it takes. People who aren't willing to aggressively chase their dreams, follow their passions, and reach their goals. Simply let it be. Don't listen to their opinion. Let them talk behind your back. Let them continue to take the same action expecting a different result, because I promise that when they look back and see how far you've come and how much you've grown, they will regret not doing so themselves. The last thing any of us want to die with, is the regret of not knowing or not doing. Go aggressively in the direction of your dreams, and don't give a damn about what anyone else thinks!

LESSON 16: BE PATIENT

~~~

It's One Of The Greatest Gifts In The World

To have love, success, and happiness all at the same time, patience is a must. The key to having patience, is learning to be a master at one thing vs. being mediocre at many things. When it comes to moving ahead and getting things done, I have very little patience because I'm quick to make decisions and aggressive to move the project ahead. However, in making quick decisions, I've learned that they aren't always the right or best decision. With a little more time and research, I could've saved myself the headache or loss of effort, energy, and money if I hadn't been so hasty and planned just a little bit better.

One of the greatest things about being in business is the ability to make decisions. Making the right decisions at the right time requires a steep learning curve, and there is no other tool you will need more in your organization and in today's businesses then patience. When I work with six-figure entrepreneurs, I often realize they themselves are doing some of the activities that are holding them back from reaching a higher level of success and adding more to their bottom line.

Steve is a coach. He's done an amazing job at building his business to where it is today. But, Steve believes that there is no one who can write his weekly newsletters faster or better, or that can convert clients higher than he can. After having a conversation with Steve, and asking him how many hours a week he spends preparing these newsletters in addition to all of his other responsibilities he says six. That's six hours of creativity, work, and time at the office that could be spent doing other far more important things. Steve built this multi-million dollar power house to where it is today but Steve didn't realize what those six hours a week were truly costing him.

After recommending that he outsource his newsletter, being very hesitant to do so, Steve agreed. This one small change has led to an additional six hours a week, 24 hours a month, and 312 hours a year of time away from the office at home with the kids or wife doing what he truly enjoys. Steve not only got his time back, but outsourcing his newsletter increased his income more than three times what it was before. Yet, Steve had been writing these newsletters for more than a decade. He had been serving clients, doing payroll, and overseeing every aspect of his operation because he was stuck in the mindset that there was no one who could do it better than he could. Steve lost massive amount of time and money and you probably are too.

We all fall into this trap in both our personal lives and our businesses. It costs money to hire people. It costs time and requires effort to train them. But, it costs more on your bottom line not to. Patience is a key factor in building a successful business. Just because you aren't leading the team, or involved in the day to day operations of the project doesn't mean that you can't make the final decision or approve the final copy before it gets sent to clients, or promoted to prospects.

Patience costs organizations millions of dollars in additional yearly revenue because we are too stubborn, stuck in our ways, frugal, or anal to give up the tasks we aren't masters at. I'll be the first to admit patience isn't one of my strong points, but it's something I've learned to overcome as my business grew and my needs changed. I don't have time to sit in front of the computer and study coding, website design, graphic design, branding, marketing, email campaigns, customer service, public relations, human resource, payroll, and all of the other tasks associated with running a business. The time it takes to not only learn the skill, but master the skill would be better spent on increasing my ability to coach and increasing my clients' results and revenue. If you're like I was, then you're probably thinking you can't afford it, it isn't worth it, or you don't have the time to find the perfect person or train them properly.

Let me assure you, it isn't as difficult as it may appear. For the longest time I was a master at being mediocre, average, content, and when I realized how many clients I was losing, how many people I wasn't serving, and how much money I was leaving on the table, I had no option but to invest in aligning myself with the right people, investing in the right tools, and trusting in my teams skills and abilities to deliver the best content, with the highest value, that would bring the greatest return for both of us. Was it easy to give up the need to want to control? Hell no! Did I want to give up the money I knew I needed to give up to train others? Hell no! Did I want to spend time training people? Not especially! But, what I realized in the process, is that there is nothing that is quicker, easier, and more effective than investing in people.

Today, both Steve and I understand this principle and use it on a daily basis. We both focus strictly on the one thing we are masters at and outsource all of the tasks we are mediocre at. Why? Because while it does cost time, effort, energy, and money, it increases our time to do other things. Increases our marketing efforts to reach more customers and add more value to the world. Increases our energy and ability to focus on doing what it is we truly love to do. More importantly, it exponentially increases our bottom line. You see not having patience to invest in yourself and your team is like shooting yourself in the foot. You can't move without help, and you can't have it all, all at the same time if you don't have someone to lean on.

Let's look at this a different way. Remember your first job? You were excited you were finally going to get paid, and you were finally going to be able to buy all of the things you wanted. In order to do that though, someone in the chain of command had to invest time, effort, and energy in training you because it wasn't just about giving you a paycheck. If that was the case you would just show up on payday and forget about showing up every other day you were scheduled to work. This investment has brought you to the point you are at in your career today, and this investment was the starting point for you to increase your knowledge, skills, and abilities. This investment wasn't an investment of time, effort, energy, or money, as much as it was an investment of patience in the hopes that there would be a return.

Patience is a gift like no other, and as you continue to accelerate in your career, add to your growing family, or give back to your community, one of the greatest skills you should learn and implement is patience. With great patience comes great rewards. The reward of teaching someone something they didn't know before. The reward of seeing the joy in their face when they master the skill. The reward of them now being able to do it on their own effortlessly and being able to show others how to do the same. The biggest reward though, is knowing that you helped them grow, and influence others in a loving, caring, and forgiving way, so they could be all that they were born to be and so much more. The most important lesson in this process though, is when you learn patience, you learn love.

LESSON 17: BE PASSIONATE

~~~

It's Contagious

As you can tell from reading this book, I am incredibly in love and passionate about what I do. I enjoy being around people and helping them bridge the gap between where they are now and where they want to be. While at the same time teaching them they can have it all, all at the same time. Love, success, and happiness. When I speak, people listen. When I tell stories, people engage. When I write books, people buy them. When I do interviews, I'm asked to be come back and be a guest again. Why? Because passion is contagious. Passion is one of the greatest qualities an individual can have. Many people aren't blessed to be able to find their passion especially when they're 22. I've been incredibly blessed, and now it's my mission to inspire others across the globe.

What is passion? It's the smile on your face. The tone in your voice. Your body language. Passion is the fire in your belly that sparks other people to take action.

Let me share with you a true story about a deal I just closed.

Thirty people were given the same opportunity. Twenty-nine were disqualified and eliminated before I showed up.

Say less. Do more. Be confident. Close the deal.

They wanted me before I even walked in or opened my mouth. Your presence is more important than your presentation.

That's passion. When people know they want to close a deal with you before the negotiating even begins, that's passion. When you can close, close to a 75K deal in 30 minutes, that's passion. When you walk into the room and everyone lights up and looks at you, that's passion. When people start asking you question after question about what you do, that's passion.

Nothing great is ever achieved without passion. You can never be too passionate. Passion is when you wake up excited to start the day. You go to bed excited about all that you have accomplished, and all that you are going to accomplish. You become excited about the people you met, the impact you made, and the value you added. Passion is an intensity. It's energizing. It's exciting. It's intensifying.

Passion is about setting goals, staying on target, and becoming the best at what you do. It's a relentless and ruthless commitment to learning. It's disciplined and focused work. Passion is about helping others achieve the levels of success they never dreamed possible. I'm absolutely committed in everything that I do to help my clients and those whose lives I'm fortunate enough to touch to get the results they want in the quickest, easiest, and most effective way possible.

There isn't a day that I don't wake up excited about my successes, and energized about what I've got planned. When people meet me, they know I'm passionate because of the way I dress, the way I talk, and the way I present myself.

People question, am I in business for love or for money? While I don't discuss money, the reality is I wouldn't be in business if I wasn't in it for money. At the same time, I wouldn't be able to make money if I didn't love what I do. Passion really is the essence of commitment. It isn't about writing down your goals and hoping that you will achieve them. It's taking the action necessary to achieve them in every single area of your life, every single day.

As you can probably tell from the words on this page, my passion runs deep, and it's extremely noticeable. While pursuing your passion isn't as simple and easy as people make it sound, it's worth every sacrifice. There's nothing I wouldn't give up to live a life of passion. It's such an amazing feeling to know your purpose and be driven by it every single day.

If you don't know what your passion is, I encourage you to find it and follow it. You won't regret it.

LESSON 18: LEAD SELFLESSLY

~~~

You Can Be One Or The Other, But Not Both: Selfish Or Successful

The most successful businesses in the world are run by leaders who are selfless. Selfless leaders put their teams and clients before themselves. You can't be selfish and successful. Business doesn't work that way.

Here's how it really works. You get lost and you keep going. You panic but you overcome. You resist but stay determined. You fail but focus.

Harry S. Truman once said, "It's amazing what you can accomplish if you don't care who gets the credit."

Apologize. This is one of the hardest things to do, especially if you're stubborn or don't think it's your fault. Apologizing is a way for you to ask forgiveness for the wrong you've done. While you may not have meant to hurt someone, you did physically, mentally, or emotionally. To help the individual overcome their temporary feelings for you, apologize. This small act of kindness can go a long way.

Respect. One of my biggest pet peeves is when people don't respect one another. Each of our time is valuable. But each of our values is different. Don't make an appointment if you aren't going to show up. If someone is having a bad day empathize. Selfless people understand that it isn't always about them.

Putting others before their own needs helps build stronger bonds with their personal and professional relationships. The respect is then oftentimes reciprocated.

Forgive. There will be things in your life that are beyond your control. Be strong and brave enough to forgive. Forgiveness is a powerful gift we were all given. It allows us to overcome hurt, anger, and hatred and move on with our lives. I'm sure at some point you've dealt with something that was less than desirable, murder, rape, cancer, loss of a loved one because of a drunk driver, suicide, or whatever. The point is that we are all humans and we all deal with these things. You weren't meant to deal with them alone. Find comfort in conversation. Allow yourself to open up to others about what is going on, and forgive yourself and others. I didn't say forget what happened. Simply forgive what happened and move on. Time heals all wounds.

Be grateful. Gratitude is one of the greatest gifts in the world. It goes a long way. It helps heal and forgive. It shows appreciation for those around you, and it opens and expands opportunities that would otherwise not exist. Individuals who achieve the greatest level of success in any area of life are grateful for all of the struggles, hardships, sacrifices, and opportunities they've been given to get to where they are. Beyond that, they are grateful for the people they've met, places they've been, and things they've seen. There isn't a single thing they aren't grateful for, because it's helped them in some way become a better person. Remember, as a leader, you can be selfish or successful but you can never be both.

LESSON 19: BE FLEXIBLE

~~~

FAIL FAST & FAIL OFTEN

There is no such thing as being perfect. The ability to fail fast and fail often allows you to shorten the learning curve, but being flexible in the process accelerates your growth. There are no shortcuts to love, success, or happiness. The only shortcut is failing fast and failing often. I was listening to a radio show the other day with Grant Cardone, who I absolutely love, and Jarrod Glandt, his co-host. The show is called, "Young Hustlers." On this particular episode, Grant called Jarrod out because he recently got into a relationship and wanted to move the lady he was dating to Florida, even though he had no idea whether the relationship would work out. While everyone was telling him not to take the risk, Grant and I were encouraging Jarrod to do the exact opposite. Take the risk. Create the opportunity, and if it doesn't work don't worry about it. Simply move on. On the other hand, if it does work you'll never regret the decision you made to act on the opportunity presented.

That's the beauty of being flexible. You will never know if the risk you are taking is going to work out. You will never know if the opportunity you accept is the right opportunity. Unless you take the risk and accept the opportunity. Many of you who read my first book, or who have listened to the countless interviews I've done, know that the contents of that book is about my relationship with an amazing man. The book starts out with "Is it even possible to fall in love in six weeks? I don't know, but if this isn't love, then I don't know what is." Rohan, my significant other has no idea the book is dedicated to him and written about us.

And, he won't know until I sit down and have that conversation with him when he gets back from working abroad.

But, I'm confident that his reaction is going to be one of shock and excitement. We were having a conversation the other day via FB message, which is the only way we communicate and I quote, "If writing books and being a celebrity is part of the process, then so be it." He doesn't care how much success I have. He isn't intimidated by titles, accolades, or money. Instead, he's genuine, authentic, caring, and confident in himself. Neither of us know if this will work out forever, but one thing is clear: If you aren't flexible, you'll never know.

When he told me he was working abroad, I could've said, "Well good luck. I don't ever want to talk with or see you again." Or, I could've said, "Thanks for putting your career before our relationship." Instead, I became flexible. Not because I had to, but because I wanted to. Flexibility in relationships, business, and other areas of life allows you to focus on what truly matters and get the results you truly want.

Numbers and timelines can be adjusted far easier than habits, disciplines, and systems. Let's look at this from a business perspective. Let's say you have a big project coming up and the deadline is fast approaching, but in order to have the best result or the result you want, you have one of two choices work harder, longer, and faster or move the deadline. Most things in life aren't do or die. Allowing flexibility in your health, finances, career, or relationships builds trust, credibility, and respect. It also provides a solid foundation for long-term growth.

If you don't take the risk, you won't know if it will work. If you aren't flexible, you won't see the results. If you aren't open to the opportunity, you could regret not taking it. Flexibility is an essential trait successful people utilize on a regular basis and I encourage you to too.

LESSON 20: BE APPROACHABLE

~~~

Make People Want To Be Around You

I just got off the phone with a professor from a university in Houston, TX. As we talked, he was encouraged that he could create a successful business at 60 years old with 20 hours a week and $400 of additional income in addition to what he was currently doing. Now he, like many people, are in a situation that is less than desirable. His daughter is going off to college next year, and retirement is fast approaching. He once had a $200,000 a year income, and now has a job that only pays $50,000. His dreams, hopes, goals, and desires are still there though.

You are never too young or too old to dream and then act on that dream. He saw a recent status update of mine on Facebook and then utilized LinkedIn to connect with me. Once I accepted his invite, he sent an email asking for my number so he could call. I didn't know this guy. I didn't know his situation. I haven't met him before, and had no idea even why he was interested in having a conversation. But, I loved that he took the time to reach out, and was bold enough to pick up the phone and call.

All too often we make an assumption that those we desire to connect with aren't available. When in fact they are we just haven't been bold enough to ask. And, if we did ask and got shut down we weren't bold enough to find someone else to ask instead. When people are bold enough no matter how successful one is or how much time one has available, generally an individual will make time to have a conversation, even if it's as short as two minutes. Those two minutes have extreme significance for the individual who asked. This acts not only as a confidence booster, but it also leaves the individual bragging about how awesome you and your company are.

I didn't have to do anything for this guy, except give him a couple minutes of my time. He thought I was going to tell him he should stick to his job and it wasn't possible for him to have it all. So, when I said the exact opposite, that I started my business on virtually nothing and have grown it from a mere idea to a full time successful business, he was even more encouraged to make the sacrifices and implement the habits and disciplines necessary to get to where he wants to be, so he can afford the things that he values most, such as putting his daughter through college.

Another great example of this is the story of Og Mandino who showed up at his own event to speak and was approached by a gentleman who had no interest in attending the event but simply wanted to purchase all of Mandino's books for his wife's birthday. His wife, who was obsessed with Mandino, thought she was getting a Toyota. Little did she know, her husband was bold enough to show up and ask for Mandino's signature.

The people who build the greatest relationships and who find the most success in whatever they do aren't the ones who are sitting on their ass waiting for their dreams to jump off paper and manifest themselves. These are the ones bold enough to go in the direction of their dreams, to ask for what they want, and to eventually get it. As a successful entrepreneur myself, no matter what I have going on, who I have to meet with, or how many client and sales calls I have to make, I find time to write. In the back of all of my books, I provide my personal contact information because I want people to know that I'm approachable. I want them to understand that I started where they are, and I only have the things I have because someone allowed me to approach and learn from them

Being approachable makes people want to be around you. It makes people want to buy from you. And, it encourages people to build their confidence and ask for things without the fear of rejection. Being approachable is a trait all great leaders have.

LESSON 21: BE TRANSPARENT

~~~

People Are Attracted To People Who Keep It Real

Transparency is an important part of leadership, and a critical part of self-growth. When you are honest with who you are, where you are now, and where you are going, then and only then will you feel comfortable and confident in sharing that with the world. You see, some of the stories I tell throughout this book I've never told before and it's not because I didn't want to, but because it's not "comfortable." Comfort is a casket and unless you are dead you should get comfortable being uncomfortable.

Making a successful business look easy is hard. Being transparent about your wins and losses, successes and failures, setbacks and setups isn't easy but it's what attracts leaders. Creating raw, relevant, and real content that people can relate to, sharing stories that encourage people to keep going regardless of their circumstances or current situation, and being 100% transparent about your life and business is what creates incredibly successful businesses that are not only profitable, but are also sustainable.

I don't have to be sharing my personal life, I don't have to be sharing my struggles in business, I don't even have to write this book, but I am, because I know it is going to help you. It's going to be the blueprint that you use just like I did to have it all, all at the same time. Love, success and happiness. I'm not going to make you believe that the journey you are about to embark on, or are currently on, is going to be easy. I'm not going to tell you that you don't need to invest mentally, physically, emotionally, and psychologically. I'm not going to give you the same story every other personal development author is giving that if you do these simple steps, your life is going to magically transform into the greatest thing that ever happened since sliced bread. The reality is, this is a lifelong commitment. It's day in and day out disciplines. It's taking massive action consistently. It isn't about a wish, hope, or dream. Many people have those, but not many people are willing to make the sacrifices long enough, endure the pain long enough, or invest more than enough to get the results that they want. That's the reality.

Like I've said before, I didn't grow up with a silver spoon in my mouth. I've had and continue to have things that get in my way. Life isn't going to be easy, but when you commit to do whatever it takes, no matter what it takes, when you declare that your life will never be the same and then start aligning your values and beliefs with your actions and results, your life will truly never again be the same. Being this open, honest, and candid is my way of paying it forward.

When I first got into business no one told me that I was going to have to create the product and programs. That I was going to be doing the marketing, selling, website development, customer service, public relations, or all of the other things that go into a business. There are far too many things to list here, and far too many hats to wear. When you embark on the endeavor of entrepreneurship, it's a ride like none other. It's amazing to see how many people give up because the going gets tough. Sure it's not easy, but I can tell you every sacrifice I've ever made was worth it, because there is no other feeling greater than the feeling of accomplishment. No one knows what goes on in the background to make success look so easy except you. So celebrate and enjoy the ride, because you were born to be amazing!

LESSON 22: BE DECISIVE

~~~

It's The Only Way To Get Clear On What You Really Want

The greatest leaders in the world make decisions and then create plans of execution surrounding those decisions. I've never seen a leader be presented with an opportunity and then choose not be decisive. We are presented with dozens of opportunities each day. The number of opportunities in comparison to the time we have is immeasurable. There are specific techniques you can use to make the right decisions at the right time to increase your energy, levels of clarity, and bottom line.

Think Out Loud. Some people may call you crazy or walk by and wonder why you are having a conversation with yourself. The reality is, no matter how crazy or silly you look talking yourself through the options, pros, cons, and benefits, it is a great way to make decisions without regret. I bet there are times you talk to yourself anyway throughout the day. Even if it isn't out loud, you're running different scenarios, and outcomes in your mind. I know, because much like yourself and the rest of the world, I have that non-stop voice in my head questioning if this is the right decision, which opportunity I should take, how many chances am I going to get again if I say no, should I say no or should I agree, and if I agree how much time, effort, energy, money, and other resources am I going to need to obligate or delegate to this project, and/or what's the time frame? The list of questions goes on and on, and the voice never shuts up. It only becomes quieter with each action you take. The point is, talking through it with not only yourself but others helps you work through the list of questions and make the decision that works best for you and your business.

Set A Time Limit. Everything has a deadline, and making decisions is no different. Knowing how long you have to make a decision is just as important, if not more important, than the decision itself. One of the greatest ways to make a decision without all the headaches, hassle, and input is to have a deadline and stick to it. Setting a time frame allows you to only replay all of the options in your head so many times. Only ask so many people. Only gather so much information. And, only think about it for so long before being forced to make a decision that works for you. Setting a deadline is not only critical in the decision making process, but it's necessary in goal setting, sales, projects, and management as well.

Take A Step Back. You may think that you need to weigh out the pros and cons, or that you need to gather the opinions of the boardroom or the office. The reality is, you can make a decision in the blink of an eye if you're ok with making a mistake or have faith in your ability to make it work. You see, making a decision doesn't require a lot of work, and often times it certainly doesn't require a lot of research. We just think we need time, when all we're really doing is increasing our stress levels while we await the day we need to make a decision. When we could have just made the decision and faced the consequences of that decision as a result.

No matter what decision you are making, there will always be a lesson. Whether the decision is as simple as picking out your clothes for the day, or signing a million dollar deal. These decisions come with consequences, and these consequences will only ever be one of two things: positive or negative. Either way, you'll have to deal with it. So don't worry about being right or being wrong. Worry about being decisive and sticking with that decision.

LESSON 23: COMMAND PRESENCE

~~~

Use Endless Energy To Capture People's Attention

Naturally everywhere I go, people know who I am and it isn't because of my title of what I've achieved, but because I'm personable. I relate to people and break down their barriers leaving them no choice but to interact and engage with me. Some people, including my own family, see it as obnoxious because they aren't comfortable speaking their mind, talking loudly, or walking up to and starting a conversation with strangers. But, I am. Not too long ago, I released my first book "Be Ballsy! How Not To Suck At Love, Success, & Happiness." If you haven't picked up a copy or read it, I highly encourage you to do so. Right after we went bridesmaid dress shopping for my sister's wedding the first time, and I was days away from releasing the book, I sat with my sister, her best friend, my mom and my aunt in a small coffee shop. We sat at the table in the far back, and I sat in the chair with my back turned to the entire shop.

We conversed for some time before I pulled out my book and read a small part of it which happened to be, in my opinion, the funniest part of the book. Not paying attention to how loud I was speaking, I open the book and started to read. My mom who was sitting in the chair next to me off to the left kept telling me to shush. Ignoring her, I continued. As she kept repeating herself over and over, I turned around and there were people listening to me read the passage and laughing. One of the guys in the booth pipes up and says, "This sounds like me. What book are you reading?".

So I start a conversation with a complete stranger telling him about my book. How it's being released on Amazon in just a few short days. He asked me to keep reading as I was semi-embarrassed that what was intended to be a conversation between those closest to me had now turned into a public conversation. I continued for a minute. Then we both continued what we were doing. Almost an hour later, as we were getting ready to leave the shop, I walked up to his booth while my family left and continued our conversation introducing myself, showing him the book, and exchanging personal contact information. As we conversed, he told me how he was there writing his own book and how they (him and the girl sitting across from him) were going through the editing process. With a stack of hundreds of papers full of red ink and corrections stacked in front of them, I could see we had much more in common than either of us anticipated.

These are the kind of situations I run into every day, because I'm not afraid to talk to people. If you're shy, I would encourage you, for the next 90 days, to walk up to someone you don't know and start a conversation. This will not only increase your comfort level, but it will also increase your confidence level and open doors and opportunities that wouldn't otherwise exist. I'm not telling you to go out of your way and do this. If you are having dinner start a personal conversation with the waiter. If you are standing in line have a personal conversation with the person standing next to you. If you are at school, start a conversation with the students around you. It will be uncomfortable at first, but as you warm up to those you interact with on a daily basis you will begin to realize how many opportunities and how much money you are leaving on the table by not doing something as simple as having a conversation.

Energy is everything. When you are happy, excited, inspired, and passionate, people recognize that and pay attention. You don't have to do anything other than be yourself to get this kind of attention either. Let me share another short story with you to illustrate this point. Christmas 2013, I was invited to a private concert with a friend. Upon arrival, I sat in the front row right in front of the mic where the artist was performing. As the concert was getting started you could feel the level of energy and excitement increasing in the auditorium. In the middle of the second song the vocalist says "I like your shoes. I really like your shoes!" I had on five inch lime green pumps. I didn't have to say or do anything to get attention. I simply had to be present and be me.

This one sentence in her performance had people swarming around me at intermission, and after the concert, asking about my shoes. The couple sitting next to me with who I had tried to converse with several times wasn't very talkative. Come to find out later, that was the mayor and his wife. I'm sure they appreciated the attention.

Energy and passion go hand in hand. You can have one without the other but when you have both it's an extremely powerful combination that draws people to you and excites people around you. I have extreme energy levels on a regular basis. In fact higher than most people. Through a simple conversation, and through the words on a page, people can feel my passion, energy, and enthusiasm for what I do. I'm extremely obsessed with personal development, and incredibly passionate about my life's purpose. No one has to drag me out of bed in the morning or ask me to burn the midnight oil. I'm happy to do so.

But the question often gets asked, "How do you maintain such high energy levels?". I'll give you a couple simple things you can do to increase your energy and live the life of your dreams. All of these tips I cover in detail throughout the pages of this book.

Hydrate. Water makes up 80% of the body and is extremely important to use as fuel to help you build and maintain the body of your dreams.

Work Out. Not only is working out great for the body, but it clears the mind. One of my favorite things about working out is throwing on my favorite music and jamming to it while getting all sweaty. Personally, I hate sweating, but somehow it becomes tolerable when I'm concentrated on singing along with the music that drives me to push harder, further, faster, and more than I've ever done before.

Meditate. Whether its guided meditation or just meditating on your own, clearing your head and focusing on nothing for a brief period of time increases your energy and provides more clarity surrounding your goals. Meditation is something I engage in every single night before falling asleep, because the last hour before you sleep and the first hour in the morning program the subconscious mind. Meditation is a great tool to help you reprogram your mind so you get the clarity you need to have it all, all at the same time.

Eat Clean. You might be surprised when I tell you that everything you use to fuel the body either increases or decreases your energy. Let's say you just go to the fridge to get something to eat. Except you're so hungry you decide to eat everything in sight, leaving you lying on the couch wondering how you're going to recover. This is what I call a food coma. You load your body with carbs, fats, and sugars, which take hours for the body to break down and process. By fueling your body with negative calorie foods, such as broccoli, cauliflower, spinach, celery, and other greens, your energy, confidence, and sex appeal automatically increase as a result. Leaving you feeling good, looking good, and getting more done in less time.

Sleep. Getting 6 to 7 hours of sleep a night will energize you far more than getting 8 or more hours. For the longest time, I believed that I needed to sleep at least 9 to 10 hours a night and I would still wake up feeling groggy, drained, and lack the energy I needed throughout the day. Once I switched my schedule and started waking up earlier but going to bed at the same time I realized how much more energy I had then I did before. Not only did my energy increase, but my productivity, clarity, and ability to get things done quicker also increased. Sleeping is necessary, but it isn't necessary to sleep all day.

Make Date Night & Sex With Your Significant Other A Priority. Not only should you make date night with your significant other a priority, you should also make sex a priority. You already know I'm not afraid to talk about sex, and I think it should be addressed because it's an important aspect of our lives and it can affect our business in a big way. If you're worried about how much time you have to spend with your partner, you aren't spending enough time with them. One of the easiest, and quickest ways to increase your energy is to converse, bounce ideas off of, and spend time having fun with your partner. Life isn't about how hard you can work. It's about the experiences you collect. Making your partner a priority should be at the top of your list. It's amazing what just spending 2-3 hours with your partner a week can do to your relationship.

I want to leave this lesson with this thought. Don't ever apologize for being you and doing what you do. While some people may think you are crazy, it's those same people that are not passionately pursuing their dreams, or making the sacrifices necessary to reach their goals. Creating more energy isn't hard, actually it's pretty easy if you follow these simple steps when you're feeling down. Remember energy is an instantly renewable resource. Doing any one of the above mentioned things will automatically increase your energy and attract others to you.

LESSON 24: BE A ROLE-MODEL

~~~

Your Actions Speak Louder Than Words

No matter what you say, or how much you say it, nothing will speak louder than your actions. Whether it comes to your children or your business, people are paying attention to the actions you are taking far more than anything you are saying and then modeling your behavior. If you have bad habits, these can easily rub off on your children, teams, and organizations. Let me give you an example. I grew up in a house where eating healthy wasn't the norm. Actually, regular trips to the store would include chips, candy, soda, hamburger, and other incredibly unhealthy processed foods that were quick and easy to make. These behaviors, because they were repeated daily for years, were then carried into adulthood. Trips to the store for one or two things, shopping carts filled with empty calories, and hours in front of the television shoving our faces full of things that weren't healthy making our bodies and bank accounts dry, were part of the daily routine.

If my parents are reading this, I'm sure they're pissed I would even share this, but the reality is the same thing is happening in your household whether you realize it or not. Sorry! This may be a little harsh, but I don't care how many speeches you've given to your children about going to the gym or eating healthy. If you aren't doing it yourself, your words are meaningless. I don't care how many times you've told your children to clean their rooms. If you aren't setting the example, they aren't listening. I don't care how many times you've told your children about being financially responsible, if you aren't doing it they won't either.

All of the habits and disciplines you've developed and display to your children influence them far more than you realize. All of the habits and disciplines you've developed in the workplace influence your team far more than you know. All of the habits and disciplines you've developed in your personal life influence your friends, family, and significant other. Let's say you're in a relationship. If your partner is fit, it isn't very likely that they are interested in their significant other being fat because they know the impact that this will have on them psychologically. This is called influence.

If you don't set the example, be the role model, or develop the habits and disciplines necessary to positively influence and impact those around you, then don't expect to have the love, success, and happiness you desire. You can't be in a semi-broken relationship and be happy. You can't shove your face full of garbage and be satisfied (literally or figuratively). You can't speak one way and act another and be successful. Life doesn't work that way.

In the simplest of transactions you can influence someone. In one transaction you can influence someone. On a daily basis you influence someone. Influence is what builds people, what builds character, businesses, and communities. Be someone others want to look up to. Want to get guidance and help from. Someone others desire to be like. The greatest leaders in the world develop the disciplines and habits necessary to lead by example and set the standards. It isn't easy for them and it won't be easy for you, but in doing so, you shape our future generations.

I challenge you to look at what standard you set in your life, family, and business. Then check if your values and beliefs are aligned with your actions and results. Only then will you know whether or not you are being a positive role model. Instead of lying to yourself about being one, change your habits and disciplines and become one.

LESSON 25: BE YOUR OWN HERO

~~~

No One Is More Important Than You

Some people think it's selfish to put yourself above others, but I say you can't give what you don't have. Therefore, you have to focus on yourself and your own needs before you can focus on helping other people. If I didn't take a relationship and sex sabbatical for nearly three years, there is no way that I would have been able to fall in love so quickly. In fact, many times we're hurt, angry, frustrated and upset that we aren't able to have what we want in life and yet we aren't willing to make the sacrifices to get that. Before I fell in love with my amazing partner, I dated on and off for years. I would go from one guy to the next without really having interest in any of them. I would always put the guy before my own needs and that never paid off.

There are several lessons I learned from this that not only applied to my own personal life but to my business as well. For three years I focused on me. Selfish? I don't think so. When I moved back into my parents' house at 21, after living on my own and having a six-figure salary, great home, brand new car, and all the freedom I wanted, I was in the worst position I had ever been mentally, physically, emotionally and financially. Three years was the length of time I needed to heal past wounds, and forgive myself for the mistakes I had made. Was it difficult? You damn right. But, I will tell you there wasn't a second of sacrifice that wasn't worth it.

I wouldn't be in the position that I am now to commit to my relationship, business, happiness, and own desires if I hadn't taken that time to be my own hero, and still continued to do so today. There is no one in the world that is more important than you are. Even if you're a parent, student, athlete, doctor, lawyer, or entrepreneur, when you put yourself first and invest in the resources you need to be your best, then and only then can you give your best to those who are counting on you. Clients, classmates, kids, and others watch what you are doing far more than they listen to what you are saying.

You and only you know whether or not you are taking the right actions and doing the right things to get the results that you truly want in your life. You can't be accountable to anyone more then you are accountable to yourself. That's why being a hero in your own life before others is critical. Let me give you an example. As a leader it's my job to inspire others to build million dollar businesses, lose weight, get in shape, increase sales, improve the bottom line and much more, but if all I'm doing is preaching instead of setting the example, then you see, I'm no longer a leader because I can't even lead one, myself.

Being your own hero is hard. I don't like being accountable to anyone, and I certainly don't like being accountable to myself, because there are times I want to give up, call it quits, or just not do what I know I should be doing. But, that's where the power of reinforcement and backup comes in. When you build an amazing inner circle, there is no way for you to get out of those tasks. Imagine this for a minute, every time you don't want to go workout or eat healthy you come up with an excuse and follow that excuse with I'll do it tomorrow, and yet tomorrow never comes.

What if instead you took away that option, and weren't able to get out of working out and eating clean because your best friend who was ruthless, and relentless about working out showed up every single morning and regardless of if you felt like doing it you had to, because you didn't want to disappoint yourself, much less your best friend. If you set yourself up for failure you will fail. However, if you set yourself up for success, you will succeed. I've learned there is no better way to be your own hero then to create amazing relationships with people who are far more committed to the journey then you are, yet started in the exact place you are.

If Matt wasn't asking me how sales were, or calling me to see how many new people were in the pipeline, if Darren wasn't holding me to my fitness goals by having me write down every single thing I put in my mouth, if Roger wasn't helping improve my vocals with warm-up exercises every morning or before I went on stage or in front of camera to speak, if I didn't have people who supported, encouraged, and demonstrated high levels of commitment to improving my performance, then I wouldn't be as driven as I am to reach my goals or meet the deadlines.

Being your own hero requires a level of investment most people aren't willing to make. It requires investing everything you have. Putting everything on the line for whatever it is you want. Being your own hero means sacrifices that require long hours, lots of money, time, effort, energy, and a willingness to do whatever it takes, no matter what it takes.

Are there days I don't want to be my own hero? Of course! But I won't, don't, and can't let that stop me, because I've been blessed with a gift no one else is given. You have been as well. If you don't commit to tapping into your full potential, investing at the highest level, or doing whatever it takes, then you can never expect to have it all.

Here's the definition of hero:

You can't be in a great relationship if you don't love yourself first.

You can't be in great shape if you don't put yourself first.

You can't be a great teacher if you aren't a great student first.

You can't find your passion if you don't take enough action.

You can't be the best if you don't invest.

I am my own hero because I want to be. I don't need to be or have to be, but I truly want to be. I want to be the person that wakes up in the morning excited about what the day holds. I want to be that person others aspire to be. I want to be the one on stage inspiring millions of people to wake up and take action so they can have it all, all at the same time. I want to be the person in the room with the most energy, attracting the most attention. I want to hold myself and my clients to the highest standards because there is nothing more powerful. I am my own hero, and I encourage you to be your own too. Whether you are aware of it or not, you are influencing through your words, and more importantly your actions, those around you. I want to leave you with this question. If you don't become great how can you expect those you love, and those you surround yourself with to be great either? Go be your own hero!

CHAPTER 8

~~~

DO WHATEVER IT TAKES

Life can knock you down sometimes. As we come to an end together, I want to share a story with you about how no matter what I had going on, no matter how many appointments I had, calls I needed to make, or things I needed to do, doing the very things I didn't want to do were the very things that have built the foundation for where I am today. There's a misconception in the world that entrepreneurs have time to do whatever they want, wherever they want, with who they want, when they want. The reality is, that's the furthest thing from the truth in the first couple years of starting a business. That is, if you can even survive the first couple years. I wasn't born with a silver spoon in my mouth, like I have stated before. My parents weren't rich, and never will be. It wasn't luck that brought me to where I am today. It was determination, an unwillingness to quit regardless of what was against me, and an unwavering faith in myself.

It was only a short time ago that I was struggling. Struggling to make money, to create a sustainable business, to engage people, to commit to what I said I wanted, and to take the action necessary to reach the goals I had. I was struggling to keep going. I wanted to give up. I wanted to quit. I wanted to sit back, relax, and chill. But, something was driving me. That something was a hunger. A desire so deep that no matter how bad I wanted to quit, give up, or take a break, I couldn't. This passion made me wake up early and stay up late. It forced me to give up everything I had so I could have everything I wanted.

In 2010 when I quit my job and moved back into my parents' house because I was broke, homeless, and hungry after being on my own, I had a decision to make. I could keep living this way or do something about it. I spent countless hours in front of the computer. I studied personal development like my life depended on it. I made phone calls I didn't want to make. I avoided the news at all cost. I would read, study, write, and speak in a way that would capture an audience and demand attention, but it wasn't easy.

Actually, it was hard as hell, because of the situation, mindset, and position I was in. I hate that my parents didn't have it easy. I hate that they couldn't go on vacation or afford what they wanted. I hate that they bought bargain brands and shopped at second hand stores, never buying new clothing for themselves. I hate that they live in a town of 350 people where eyes are constantly on them. I hate that their house is nothing to brag about. I hate that they have to kill themselves working damn near seven days a week and still barely have enough money to pay the bills. I hate that they have to pay ridiculous APR's because they have to finance everything. I hate that they have to live a life like that. I hated it so much it would reinforce my passion and desire to create something better for myself and my family. It has literally driven me to do whatever it takes!

It wasn't until June 14, 2011 that I figured out what I wanted to do, and realized how committed to doing it I actually was. And, it was then that I was willing to give up everything I had so I could have more. It wasn't easy and it wasn't cheap. You see, I sold my dining room furniture to my brother. The same furniture I loved and had paid thousands for two years earlier. I sold my black leather, seven piece living room set, that was in near perfect condition to some guy on Craigslist for about a third of what I paid for it. I made and sold t-shirt quilts for $150 via FB even though I had far more than $150 in time invested into them. I sold my whole wardrobe, and kept a couple pairs of shoes, a couple shirts, and one pair of jeans. I gave up my whole life, everything I knew, and had seen as security to follow this passion and make this dream a reality. Today, I've been blessed to say that everything has paid off.

Some of the things I've done people would never do because it's incredibly hard, very expensive and extremely painful. But, I've been blessed to endure against all odds. I've been sued by creditors. I've had leans put against me. I've had my wages garnished. I've had thousands of dollars in student loans. I've been in college and dropped out of college. I've had six-figure salaries and great jobs and had no income and no job. I've been to jail for speeding. I've been on food stamps. I've lived at rest stops in Chicago on I-80 for 30 days using a washcloth as a shower, and living out of the cardboard boxes in my trunk, while sleeping in the back seat of a car I knew was up for repo. I've then had my car repo'd and lived without a car for nearly two years. I've relied on my parents to put food on the table, keep a roof over my head, keep the house warm, and the bills paid.

This is the kind of life no one wants to live but very few people have the willingness to endure and eventually live the life they want. The people who have this life rarely have strength to carry on, and the ones who do carry on become an amazing example for others. Most people in my situation would give up, call it quits, and leave even more frustrated and upset than before. I didn't have or see that as an option. I couldn't give up on my family. I refused to settle for average and mediocre. Being good enough, wasn't good enough. I wasn't aiming to be the brightest, smartest, most successful, or richest person around I was aiming to be the best me I knew I could be. I was willing to let absolutely nothing keep me from doing what I wanted to do, reaching the goals I wanted to reach, and fulfilling the dream I wanted to fulfill.

I would do anything to make my business work (that was ethical and legal of course). In 2012 my brother Max graduated high school and would take scrap metal, transmission pieces, old car parts, or whatever he could find and weld it together to make animals, statues, sculptures, and other unique pieces of art (http://www.facebook.com/maxkrivachekdesign). It was unlike anything I had ever seen and while he was busy building I knew that with my six years of experience in sales, marketing, and customer service, together we could turn what was his hobby into a full-time business.

While he was at the shop welding, I would take pictures and post them on Facebook in "For Sale" groups. Then people would come to our house and buy the stuff sitting in our back yard. I was in desperate need of money to continue growing my business, and I refused to get a job. Even if I were to get a job, which my family desperately wanted, it was miles from where I lived and I had no transportation to get there. So, I got creative and we negotiated a deal where I would get 10% of the sales price for anything I sold. 10% wasn't much, but it was enough of an incentive and a motivation to sell more. What started as online sales exploded and demanded more and more of our attention.

Giving this my attention was now costing me time and money, but I was in the mindset that without money I couldn't make money. My brother had mentioned that he wanted to have a booth at a county fair, but he didn't take the action necessary to make that happen. However, with one phone call, I did. We not only did one fair, but we did multiple back to back events over the course of three months in brutal heat. It was boring, it was mundane, it was hotter than hell, it was the same routine for 90 days, and man was it hard work.

We got a box truck, woke up early, loaded up thousands of pounds of metal sculptures tying them down and making sure they wouldn't break, and we would arrive early and unload. Then we would sit all day in the blistering sun under the grandstands at a race track on the fairgrounds, where thousands of people would pass through and look. At the end of the night we would have to be the last to leave, again loading thousands of pounds of metal sculptures. Over the course of 90 days during the hottest months of the year we sat for hours and days at six events, at which point I ended up with heat exhaustion.

During these 90 days, I barely had time to focus on my own business. Yes, I was making money, but it wasn't anything to brag about, but more importantly I was learning an invaluable lesson. No matter where you are right now, if you have the willpower, you can make it work. I spent time bonding with my little brother and his girlfriend, met some unique individuals, increased my sales skills, and levels of patience.

It didn't end there though, because we had accomplished so much in such a short period of time that I wanted him to get more recognition. So, I contacted the newspapers, and other media outlets. He was then on the front page of multiple papers and had the opportunity to be featured on KWWL, a local news station, as "Someone You Should Know." He was proud. I was proud. Together this experience was something neither one of us will ever forget.

Did I want to load thousands of pounds of sculptures twice a day, every day? Hell no!

Did I want to go to bed at midnight and wake up at 6 a.m. every day? Hell no!

Did I want to be the first to arrive at the fair, and the last to leave the fair, every day? Hell no!

Did I want to sweat my ass off, literally for 90 days? Hell no!

Did I want to sit in the scorching heat on a lawn chair for hours? Hell no!

Did I want to drink a ridiculous amount of water? Hell no! I hated water.

Did I want to be under a grand stand listening to pageants, demolition derbies, rodeos, and talent competitions without being able to participate or see it? Hell no!

Did I want people to know that I was living back in the area? Hell no! Absolutely not!

Did I want to work that hard just to make 10%? Hell no! Hell No! Did I say Hell No?!?

BUT, giving up, quitting, pulling back, or staying stuck wasn't an option. Letting myself and my family down wasn't an option. Sacrificing short-term so I could have what I wanted long-term wasn't an option. Giving up my time, spending my energy, putting in the effort wasn't an option. For me this passion, drive, commitment and dedication to personal growth and breaking through limiting beliefs was do or die.

Today, I've been fortunate enough to take those experiences, lessons, knowledge, and discipline and create a successful business. I've been blessed to move into my dream home, buy whatever I want, travel whenever I want, and have relationships with some of the most amazing leaders in the world. I've been able to share my story and experiences in a way that transforms people's limiting beliefs so they too can have it all, all at the same time. Just like I have. Love, Success, & Happiness.

I've been called a "prodigy" by Jack Zufelt, author of "The DNA of Success" and recipient of the Presidential Medal of Merit by President George Bush. I've been offered my own radio show twice, have booked and done 17 interviews in the last month, and have just finished writing two books in 56 days. I've been on the same shows and tele-summits with the people I studied and looked up to for so long; Bob Burg, Pat Flynn, Dr. Tony Allesandra, Larry Winget, Gary Barnes and countless others. I've built relationships with people most only dream of. I've been able to spread my message through my unique ability to tell stories that resonate and captivate leaders and audiences across the globe.

I'm not telling you this to brag, but to simply show you what is possible in less than three years at 25 years old. I've been incredibly blessed to find and follow my passion at such a young age. I've only been able to do this because of my unwavering commitment to succeed. This journey has been a rollercoaster. It's had ups and downs, bends and loops. It's been smooth in some spots and jerky in others.

If you're ready to have it all this is the requirement. You must:

- Do whatever it takes.
- Never give up no matter how much pain you endure.
- Be willing to pay the price.
- Be willing to sacrifice short-term to get what you want long-term.
- Be willing to give up everything you know.
- Believe that you have what it takes.
- Be disciplined.
- Take MASSIVE, consistent action.
- Put yourself first.
- Invest significant time, effort, energy, and money into learning, growing, and experimenting.
- Listen to your heart.
- Be willing to put up with the crap people tell you about how they couldn't do it and neither can you.
- Stay committed and push yourself to extreme levels mentally, physically, emotionally, & psychologically.
- Change your physiology.

- Relearn everything you think you know, because chances are, everything you know isn't anywhere near close to the truth.
- Know that the only limits you have are the limits you put on yourself.
- Be driven by passion.
- Stay focused regardless of the temporary setbacks, limiting beliefs, or your current location and situation.

You must be willing to give your all, and only then can you have it all! All at the same time. Love, Success & Happiness.

As we come to the end and part ways, I want to leave you with this simple thought. You have a decision to make, and only you can make that decision.

Go Be A Baller!

~~~

Whether you received Be A Baller! as a gift, borrowed it from a friend, or purchased it yourself, we're glad you read it. We think you will agree that Melissa Krivachek is a refreshing voice, and we hope you will share this book and her thoughts with your family and friends.

If you are interested in writing to the author, wish to receive updates, or are interested in coaching with or having Melissa speak at your event or for your organization please contact us by:

Call/Text: 563-419-1101
E-Mail: melissa@melissakrivachek.com
Website: http://www.melissakrivachek.com

Connect with us on Social Media:

Facebook: http://www.facebook.com/melissakrivachek
YouTube: Search Melissa Krivachek
LinkedIn: http://www.linkedin.com/in/melissakrivachek

Everyone at some point in their life has been hurt and to a degree that keeps them in a coma like state for some time; more often than not years wondering how they could have changed, made things better or did things differently. Death, divorce and devastation are things we all deal with in our own ways. No one is invincible to these experiences.

I have experienced all of these and have become incredibly successful as a result. Today I spend my time writing, keynote speaking to audiences across the globe as well as holding small masterminds at my home.

There are a few departing words I want to conclude with; radical change starts with a decision and is followed through with a commitment.

Over the past decade I have experienced more than most people ever will in their lives and it is why I teach people to radically change their mindset, actions and results. Those choices are often the most difficult to make but have the highest impact.

As I previously mentioned early on in this book I grew up in a town of 300 people in Fort Atkinson, Iowa. From there I have been homeless on the streets of Chicago, had my car repossessed, got fired from a Fortune 500 company, been evicted, had a gun put to my head, and have spent six days in jail for speeding.

I have had it all and I have had nothing. I have been in love and I have been crushed by the pain of love.

Today I use myself as an experiment to see what works and what does not while teaching people how to make radical and more importantly sustainable changes in their lives. Let me explain when I first started my company I had no more than five cents to my name since that time over seven years ago I have taught people how to generate over 1.5 million dollars in revenue in less than twelve months from nothing but an idea.

Radical change in my life is an ongoing thing; death, divorce and devastation will always be things we as humans deal with. Just as love, success, happiness and fulfillment are things we all strive for.

Three years ago I had never written a book and did not know a single thing about it now I have published eight; five of those are on the international best-seller list. One of those is the book you have in your hands.

I struggled with my weight for years before shedding more than 130 pounds in twelve months.

I had never built a business before and now I have a very successful global brand.

Melissa Krivachek Companies

Helping People Create Radical Change

I had never stepped foot in India before I gave everything away, risked it all, got on a plane and landed in a third world country where I would not just vacation but I would live.

Radical change starts with the truth. It starts with the acknowledgement of where one is and a burning desire to go somewhere different. If you want to see radical change you must be the radical change. If you want to be radically changed you must first see that in your mind, make a decision and commit to doing those things required to get you to your goal.

Change is made in a moment, although it takes many of us years to get to that moment.

If you have ever wanted to make a radical change I would love to extend an invitation to work with you to do so.

To get an exclusive invitation to mastermind at my home head over to www.melissakrivachek.com to apply OR just pick up the phone and call our offices at 1.563.419.1101.

To have me keynote or do a break out session for your next event please call our offices at 1.563.419.1101.

I hope we get the opportunity to work together because I would love to help you radically change your life and business!

I LIVE.

I LOVE.

I HAVE BEEN HURT.

I REGRET NOTHING.

I WILL DO IT AGAIN.

ABOUT THE AUTHOR

~~~

Melissa Krivachek travels the world writing, coaching and keynoting using her story to inspire millions of people who have experienced devastation, death and divorce; people who are stuck in the same cycle wanting to make a radical change!

Made in the USA
Columbia, SC
02 August 2017